SILVER ISLET

SILVER ISLET

STRIKING IT RICH IN LAKE SUPERIOR

ELINOR BARR

Silver Islet: Striking it Rich in Lake Superior
Elinor Barr
Edited by Vivian Webb

Published by Natural Heritage/Natural History Inc.
P.O. Box 95, Station O
Toronto, Ontario M4A 2M8

© Copyright 1988
Natural Heritage/Natural History Inc./Elinor Barr

No portion of this book, with the exception of brief extracts for the purpose of literary review, may be
reproduced in any form without the written permission of the publishers.

Design: Derek Chung Tiam Fook
Printed and Bound in Canada by Mothersill Printing, Bowmanville, Ontario

Ist Printing – March 1988
2nd Printing – July 1995

Originally published with the assistance of the Ontario Heritage Foundation, Ontario Ministry of Culture
and Communications.

Canadian Cataloguing in Publication Data
Barr, Elinor
Silver Islet

(The Canadian shield series)
Bibliography: p.
Includes index.
ISBN 0-920474-41-1

1. Silver Islet Mine (Ont.) – History
2. Silver mines and mining – Ontario – Silver Islet – History.
I. Title   II. Series
TN434.C32S54 1988   338.2'7421'0971312   C86-093928-6

Natural Heritage/Natural History Inc. gratefully acknowledges the assistance of the Canada Council, the
Ontario Arts Council, and the Government of Ontario through the Ministry of Culture, Tourism and
Recreation.

To the residents and friends of Silver Islet.

CONTENTS

PART 1

PROLOGUE

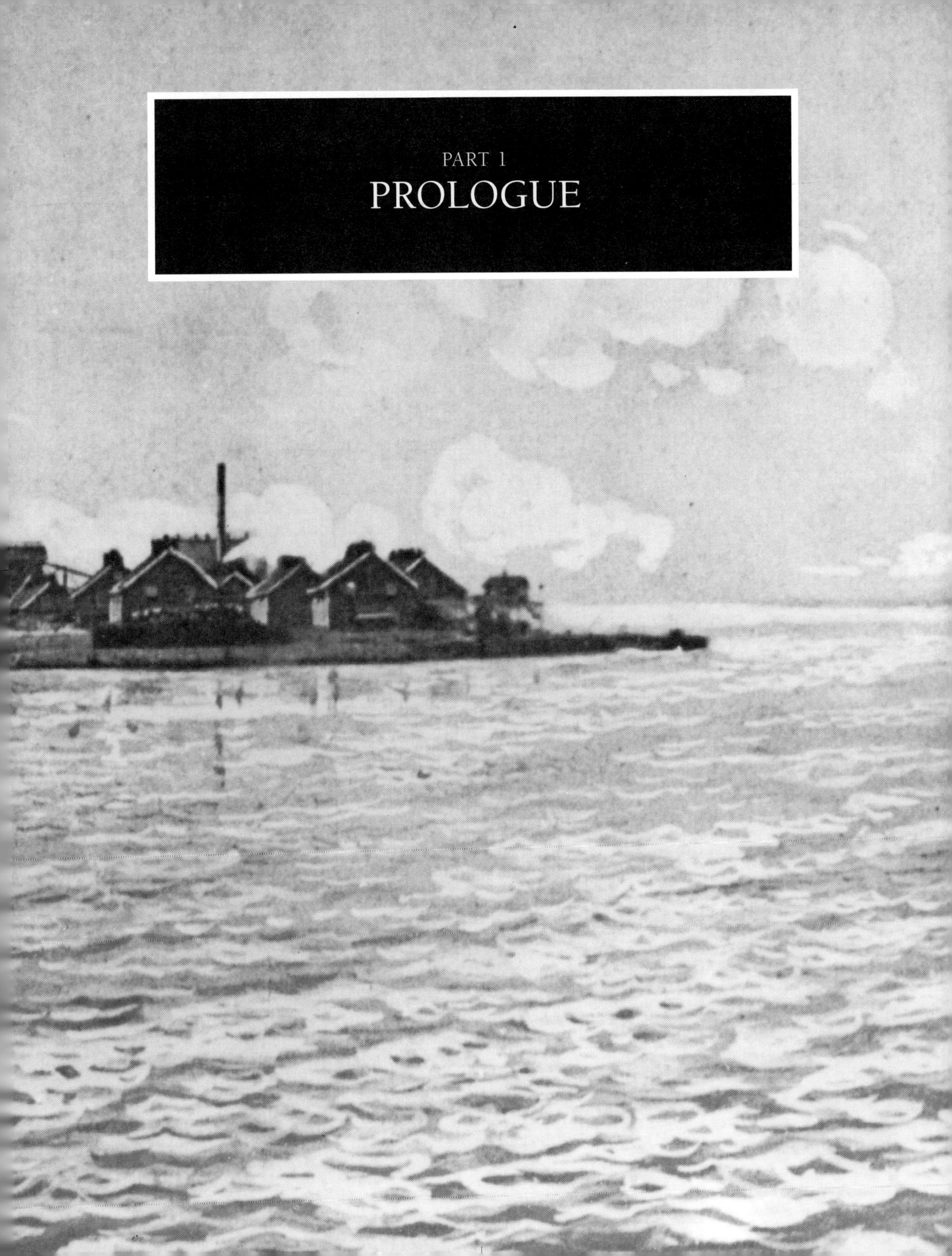

CHAPTER 1

AN UNUSUAL SETTING

John Morgan stopped short at the water's edge and knelt quickly. Nuggets of pure silver winked back at him from their rocky prison. His unbelieving eyes followed the vein, a chalk white ribbon flecked with black patches of metallic silver that glistened invitingly beneath the watery ripples.

Silver Islet ore was exceedingly rich. Thomas Macfarlane, leader of the exploration team for the Montreal Mining Company, had the packing ore assayed and his figures show the ore ranging between 2.76 percent and 5.503 percent silver. When the operation closed in 1884 the Silver Islet Mine had yielded 2,589,134 ounces (80,530 kg) of silver worth $3,250,000, averaging $1.26 an ounce. The price of silver on the New York market would not reach these heights again until the 1960s.

A more precarious perch for Canada's first successful mine would be difficult to imagine. A line drawn from end to end of Silver Islet measured no more than 90 feet, the distance a batter sprints to reach first base. Running all the bases would encircle the entire land form. On windy days whitecapped waves lapped the sloping shoreline, threatening to wash right over the islet's low curving surface. And when Lake Superior unleashed one of its furious storms, savage billows hurled themselves against the defenceless dome again and again until it seemed to sway under the attack.

The spectacular storms coming off the lake gave the area its name and were the first obstacle for the developers of Silver Islet to overcome. At first the name Thunder Bay referred only to the harbour protected by Sibley Peninsula. Early French maps record it as *baie du tonnèrre*, a translation of the Ojibway *animikie wekwid* meaning thunderbird.

> The Indians have a legend that the thunder is a huge bird having its home on Thunder Cape, where it hatches the lightnings. They say that a thunderstorm in the Bay is something terribly grand, each mountain sending back the thunder peals in deafening reverberations.[1]

The most imposing cliff face overlooking the bay rises 800 feet (243m), the highest in Ontario.

The sheer cliffs ending at Thunder Cape not only produce marvellous echoes, their outline on the horizon resembles a person lying down with his arms folded across his chest. Several vantage points within the city limits of Thunder Bay offer stunning views of the Sleeping Giant or Nanabijou*. Climbers on Sibley Peninsula who scale the Giant's knees can actually see Silver Islet on the lake side.

The Sleeping Giant as seen from Port Arthur.

Nanabijou is a popular figure in Ojibway mythology. Tales of his superhuman feats and human foibles have fascinated listeners for centuries. But the story of his being turned to stone for revealing the secret of Silver Islet Mine has a distinctly modern flavour.

The strategy adopted by the superintendent, William Bell Frue, to protect the islet from the storms' fury and to bring Silver Islet Mine into production was to cover the vein with a platform as broad as a baseball field and as high as its bleachers. This massive, timber-girdled fortress of stone acted not only as a breakwater but also as a foundation for the headframe and hoisting machinery that marked the entrance to the mine.

The superstructure was a remarkable engineering feat for the time. Only a few years earlier, in 1867, Chicago completed construction of North America's first subaqueous tunnel. Building a city waterline of brick beneath Lake Michigan's muddy floor imposed a far different set of challenges than protecting Silver Islet's vertical mineshaft. The mine's superstructure guarded a treasure trove, the only exit for underground miners and the ore they extracted. It had to be strong enough to withstand wind-driven ice as well as to support an industrial complex of immense proportions.

The townsite lay almost a mile away on the mainland, a village of single-file

* Alternate spellings include Nanabozho, Nanabush, and Nanna Bijou.

houses hidden behind the protective finger of Burnt Island. The distance from the Catholic church at one end to the President's mansion at the other measured less than six city blocks, yet during the early 1870s employees of Silver Islet Mine represented the largest concentration of people on the Canadian side of Lake Superior.

Turning of the sod for the Canadian Pacific Railway in 1875 transformed nearby Fort William from a minor fur trade post to a bustling boomtown and the future site of Port Arthur into a busy service centre. The growth of both frontier communities soon outdistanced that of Silver Islet, to which they owe a considerable debt. By focusing worldwide attention on the area's mining potential at a time when transportation patterns were being decided, Silver Islet Mine provided the impetus for the city of Thunder Bay to become the economic centre it is today.

Canada ranks as one of the world's top mine producers of silver, but much of the romance associated with mining ventures such as Silver Islet has disappeared. About 80 percent of Canada's silver comes as a by-product of base metal mining.

The enduring importance of the Silver Islet Mine rests on the richness of its ore, its maritime location and the bravery and ingenuity of the men who brought it into production. Some of these miners remain nameless, like the explorer who donned a deep sea diving outfit in 1872 in order to follow the vein's underwater course. Others remain faceless, like the hundreds of men upon whose labour the mine's production depended. But the three superintendents qualify as minemakers by any standards. Their terms of office coincided so closely with the mine's development that the story falls naturally into three sections: exploration under Thomas Macfarlane, and production under William Bell Frue and Richard Trethewey who supervised extraction of the first and second bonanzas. In this book, each section opens with a short profile of these outstanding men.

CHAPTER 2

COPPER AND SILVER

T he mining potential of the Lake Superior area began to excite official interest in 1845. That fall a United States firm sent a preliminary shipment of copper ore from its new mine on the Keweenaw Peninsula of upper Michigan. The news touched off North America's first mining boom.

Initial exploration of the area had followed hard on the heels of a glowing account of its mining potential presented to the Michigan Legislature by state geologist Douglass Houghton. William Logan of the Canadian Geological Survey reported in 1843 that Houghton's discovery was "likely to become of considerable economic value, and it remains to be ascertained", he added cautiously, "whether an analogous condition of circumstances may not extend to Canada."[1]

Although geologists of the day considered Lake Superior to be a huge east-west trough separating similar rock formations, they had not had the time or the opportunity to test their theory. In 1845 the Geological Survey had been in existence only three years and Lake Superior was remote, a faraway area associated with the Hudson's Bay Company. Other priorities clamoured more loudly for Logan's attention, especially since the then Province of Canada had not yet drafted regulations to cover mining.

The situation changed abruptly when Canadian investors responded to the copper boom by petitioning the government for permission to explore Canada's north lakeshore for minerals. One hundred and sixty such applications sat on official desks as 1845 drew to a close. Suddenly mining became a priority and Logan's advice was eagerly sought.

Before 1846 ended 27 licences were granted after a series of mining regulations were passed as orders-in-council. Each successful applicant received a generous ten-square-mile location earmarked as having mining potential. Each paid a share of the survey costs as a first instalment.

The property that included Silver Islet went to Joseph Woods[2] of Chatham, Ontario. The Woods Location, like the others, had been personally inspected by Logan. During the summer of 1846 he scouted the entire north shore by canoe, making on-the-spot decisions, taking notes, and collecting specimens of rock.[3] Travelling separately was John MacNaughton, the land surveyor appointed by the government to lay out official boundaries for each location.

Chemist T. Sterry Hunt assayed the specimens on their arrival at Montreal.

After examining the assay results, Logan concluded that the best potential lay in copper rather than any other mineral. Although several of the specimens contained traces of silver, "the quantity appeared scarcely sufficient in any instance to warrant its separation from the copper."[4] He held out hope of richer finds, however, because the silver was irregularly diffused and occurred in its native state.

Logan often stressed the superficial nature of his inspection, covering as it did only a narrow band along the coast. Nevertheless his report identified both the hard diabase dike that forms Silver Islet and the fault that crosses it.[5]

The dike can best be imagined as a petrified monster lying on the lakebottom parallel to the shoreline, facing southwest. At the precise point where its arched back breaks the surface to form Silver Islet, the monster appears to have been whacked in half, the tail portion sliding downwards in a northwest-trending dislocation, in which lies the silver deposit.

This dislocation or fault line, as it is called, extends across Burnt Island to the mainland and is most evident above the head of the Sleeping Giant, where a depression between Sawyer's Bay and Perry's Bay nearly severs Thunder Cape from the rest of Sibley Peninsula.

The Montreal Mining Company examined the Woods Location in 1846 too. The company's land surveyor, A. Wilkinson, identified three veins. Two of them ran the length of Burnt Island and Shangoina* Island, about a mile to the southwest, along the southwest-northeast direction of the dike that forms Silver Islet. The third cut the Burnt Island vein transversely along the fault line.

The Montreal Mining Company was one of several groups hastily pulled together to finance an independent study of locations under licence. The trustees appointed to carry out the company's affairs chose a Connecticut mining engineer named Forrest Shepherd to head the expedition. Governor George Simpson of the Hudson's Bay Company, one of the trustees, prepared the way by instructing his fur trade posts to assist with supplies and communication.

Shepherd's correspondence with the official in charge of Fort William, John McKenzie, underscores the extent of his dependence on these posts, the only centres of white population.

Thank you for your kindness in forwarding my papers - this offer of fresh meat fishing nets &c. Have built 12 or 14 houses & cabins on Locations. Am doing tolerably.[6]

The excerpt comes from a letter dated may 18. A month later he wrote for another fish net, one with a finer mesh, and asked for a little tea and sugar.

*pronounced Shaginaw.

"Many of my men are also barefoot," he complained. Eighteen locations were examined that summer.

Shepherd, like Logan, noted the fault line on the Woods Location. His report ended with the comment "This tract is well worthy of minute and faithful exploration." Offshore islands were important, he felt, but only insofar as they offered good harbours and visible ore veins. One of them, likely Burnt Island, he singled out as having a very prominent vein of copper crossing it:

> This vein as well as others should be traced to the highlands in the back ground of the location, and the great dislocation ... thoroughly examined, as being the repository of valuable ores.[7]

North of the fault the shoreline changed abruptly to limestone and sandstone, rocks he described as suitable for mining purposes and easily transported by water. Assay results printed in the report did not include specimens from the Woods Location.

The Province of Canada incorporated the Montreal Mining Company by statute on July 28, 1847. Joseph Woods, like 17 other licencees, assigned his location to the company under arrangements made the previous year. Little did he realize that the location would immortalize his name.

The Montreal Mining Company failed to develop the Woods Location or any of the other lands on Lake Superior that year. Instead a copper outcrop on Lake Huron absorbed all its attention. At Bruce Mines the problems of supply and communication loomed less large. Population centres were closer and more accessible. A number of merchants set up shop nearby despite company protests.

Only after completion of the Sault Ste. Marie canal in 1855 did the company turn its attention once again to the Lake Superior area. That year United States companies on the south shore shipped more than 3,000 tons of copper ore through the canal, and came close to doubling that figure in 1856.[8]

The government of Canada issued patents to the Montreal Mining Company for 16 locations, a total of about 160 square miles, at half the lowest price charged any other purchaser. The patent for the Woods Location is dated September 10, 1856 and covers ten square miles as surveyed by John MacNaughton a decade earlier.

MacNaughton had planted a cedar post "supported by three syenite boulders" near Tee Harbour, and another one at Middlebrun Bay, to mark the location's length of five miles. The two-mile depth was adjusted, in the words appearing on the patent, "so as with the small Islands in front of the lands herein described ... to include an area of ten square miles." Silver Islet appears on the accompanying plan as Island No. 4.

That silver ore existed in the Thunder Bay area was no secret. Logan mentioned finding silver on several locations. In 1846-47 the British North American

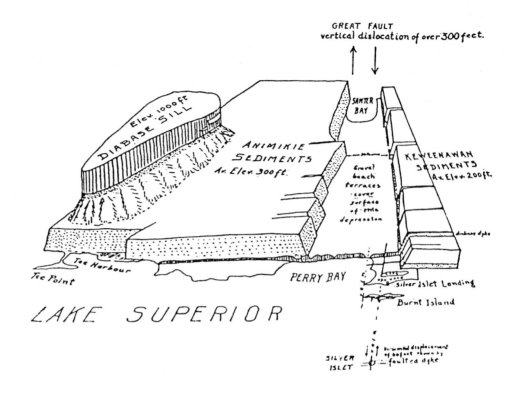

The fault line, or dislocation, crossing Silver Islet is responsible for the rich deposit of silver there.

Company extracted what was described as "a small quantity of copper-silver ores" from the Prince Location southwest of Thunder Bay. Then in 1852 certain parties at Bruce Mines sponsored a trip to Thunder Bay accompanied by a man named Secord. Secord had recalled spotting a vein of silver while employed with Bayfield's boundary survey 28 years earlier. However its exact location eluded the expedition, and Secord, disappointed and disgraced, committed suicide soon afterward.[9]

Why anyone would sponsor such a search in 1852 remains a mystery. Both silver and gold were Royal metals, so called because they were traditionally reserved to the Crown. It was not until 1866 that the reservation on silver was withdrawn. This move prompted a series of silver discoveries, some of them within the present city limits of Thunder Bay.

Peter McKellar found the north shore's first silver mine in September 1866. Since the vein lay inland from Thunder Bay, he called it Thunder Bay Mine. The previous year he and his brother, Donald, discovered the Enterprise lead mine on Black Bay, at the base of Sibley Peninsula. These finds represented the first of several important mineral discoveries by the McKellar brothers.[10]

The McKellar family lived along the Kaministiquia River, one of the few white families to settle on the north shore. In contrast, the south shore could boast a population of almost 20,000 people as early as 1860. That year United States production of copper ore stood at 8,614 tons valued at $2½ million.[11]

Peter McKellar had moved from southern Ontario to the Ontonagon copper country of upper Michigan in 1855, when he was 17. Now aged 28 and a mining entrepreneur seeking capital, he naturally compared the mining regulations of the two countries. He became convinced that the Canadian system of a 10 percent royalty on production turned away investors, especially those from the United States who were accustomed to paying a land tax of only two cents an acre.

The richness of the Thunder Bay Mine attracted many interested visitors, including a group of Ontario legislators headed by the Hon. Stephen Richards, Commissioner of Crown Lands. McKellar took the opportunity to air his views during their tour of the mine.

A land tax, he argued, would speed development and increase production, adding that the very word royalty offended republican sensibilities.[12] His speech had an impact. The ensuing Mining Act of 1868 included the hated royalty, but an amendment the following year replaced it with a tax on mining lands.

This land tax is often cited as the reason the Montreal Mining Company decided to inspect its Lake Superior locations once again. Certainly a tax of two cents an acre, to a landowner of more than 100,000 acres, represented a considerable annual assessment. However it was the previous year, in 1868, that Thomas Macfarlane was hired to carry out the work.

The impelling reason for the move may well have been the dramatic discoveries around Thunder Bay, the very area in which the company's locations were concentrated, and the possibility of recouping their initial investment. In any case, Macfarlane would meet a far different set of circumstances than Logan and Shepherd had faced 22 years earlier.

PART II

UNDERWATER OF ALL PLACES

Thomas Macfarlane (1834–1907)
supervised development of the Silver Islet vein
from 1868 to 1870.

THOMAS MACFARLANE (1834-1907)

Thomas Macfarlane belongs to that select group of well educated Scots who emigrated before Confederation and helped shape Canada's destiny within the British Empire. Despite his other accomplishments, today he is best remembered as leader of the exploration team that discovered the Silver Islet vein.

Macfarlane graduated as a mining engineer from the oldest and most prestigious mining school of his day, the Royal Mining Academy in Freiburg, Germany. He was fluent in English, German, Danish and French and travelled widely in Europe and America.

He wrote important articles for scholarly mining journals, a travel account titled *To The Andes* (1876) and an essay "Within The Empire" (1891) in support of the Imperial Federation Movement. He introduced changes in the process of smelting copper and silver ores and patented one of them as Canada Patent No. 2889, "New and Useful Improvement on the Art of Extracting Copper from its Ores by the Humid Process". He was a Fellow of the Royal Society of Canada in 1882 and served as president of the chemical section. He supervised the operation of mines in Norway, Canada and Leadville, Colorado, and attended the Third Commercial Congress in London, England in 1896. He was a mining engineer of wide and varied experience and presented influential testimony at the second Select Committee (1884) hearings on the Geological Survey of Canada.

Both Macfarlane and his wife, Margaret Skelly, came from Pollockshaws, Renfrewshire. It was the copper mines of Quebec's Eastern Townships that attracted the couple to Canada in 1860. As manager of the Acton Copper Mine, he had easy access to Montreal, Canada's foremost commercial centre as well as the home of the Geological Survey.

During the summer of 1865 he led the Geological Survey's exploration of both Hastings County and the northeast shore of Lake Superior. For three seasons, 1868-70, he headed the Montreal Mining Company's survey of its vast shoreline holdings on Lake Superior and began development of the Silver Islet vein. Despite his strong recommendation that the company bring the mine into production, the directors decided to sell.

The sale of Canada's first silver mine to United States investors must have rankled, given Macfarlane's strong imperial feelings. Nevertheless he worked as assayist for the new owners and also as manager of their Wyandotte Smelting and Refining Works near Detroit. The closest he came to censuring the transaction was in an article published in 1879 under the title "Silver Islet": "Its story ought to teach Canadians, among other things, to have more confidence in the mineral resources of their country", he wrote.

Silver Islet mine had closed in 1886 when he finally gained a permanent position with the federal government as Chief Analyst for the Inland Revenue and Customs departments. That year the family moved to Ottawa. After a long and distinguished career, Macfarlane died there June 10, 1907.

CHAPTER 3

A PROMISING VEIN

T he Dominion of Canada was less than a year old when on May 16 Thomas Macfarlane rounded Thunder Cape aboard the first steamship of the 1868 season. The sidewheeler *Algoma* drew alongside the Thunder Bay silver mine's new dock of cribwork filled with stone, just east of Current River. Here 25 miners disembarked with their supervisor, a Mr. McDonald from England. Under his shouted instructions they began unloading mining machinery, including a stamp mill, as well as food, tools and building materials. It was Mr. McDonald's task to open the mine.

Macfarlane took advantage of the opportunity to acquaint himself and his crew of Montrealers with local conditions. The little group hiked three miles inland to the minesite* to see for themselves the nature of silver veins and the ore extracted from them. Peter McKellar described the vein as "a wonderful show of silver", both native silver and silver glance.

Next the party cut overland, crossing Current River, to a second strike called Shuniah Mine. Shuniah is the Ojibway word for silver, and likely derived from the English word shilling, a British silver coin.

Here they were able to go underground since miners had already sunk two shafts, one to 60 feet and the other to 40 feet. Work had stopped only recently. The ore assayed at a mere $200 to $300 a ton, hardly worth the cost of extracting it.

The Montrealers then packed tents, tools, a portable forge and other gear into their mackinaw boat and headed southwest along the shore. No doubt Macfarlane touched bases with John McIntyre, post manager at Fort William. It would be more than a polite gesture. McIntyre was as involved with mining as his neighbours Peter McKellar and George McVicar, the discoverer of Shuniah Mine. Since the latter's sister, Christina McVicar, acted as postmaster, Macfarlane likely discussed mail arrangements with her at the same time.

First stop was the Jarvis Location, next door to the property that produced "copper-silver ores" in the 1840s, the Prince Location. Macfarlane hoped for a similar find. By the end of May he had forwarded specimens to Montreal from one of five promising veins on Jarvis Island, which fronted the Location.

Members of the crew took on whatever task he assigned. Campbell Brown

* The Terry Fox Lookout is a nearby modern landmark for the location of Thunder Bay Mine.

was the man who spotted native silver in the Jarvis island vein, but he doubled as the party's cook during most of the summer. His brother, Gerald, usually ran the survey lines. While carrying out these duties a month later on Silver Islet, Gerald Brown noticed the vein that led to discovery of silver there.

Macfarlane's party arrived at the Woods Location on June 24 after spending three disappointing weeks near Pigeon River exploring the Stuart Location. He chose a sheltered campsite and prepared for an extended stay. Logan's report had convinced him that the Woods Location warranted close inspection and careful mapping.

Accordingly his men, now reduced to four following a stop at Fort William, pitched tents in the sheltered cove that became known as Camp Bay. They also built a shanty roofed with bark where Macfarlane conducted tests on ore samples and stored his specimens and assay equipment.

On the first day he examined the shoreline west of camp, following closely behind Gerald Brown who planted survey pickets all the way to Perry's Bay. Meanwhile John Morgan and Patrick Hogan cut a line eastward. The second day the party cruised the shoreline in their mackinaw boat, visiting Islands No. 1, 2 and 3 and planting pickets as far as the location's western boundary.

The sidewheeler Algoma *rounds Thunder Cape en route to Prince Arthur's Landing.*

The third day, June 27, they finally set foot on Island No. 4:

A few square yards only of the islet, at its highest part, six feet above the level of the lake, shew any traces of vegetation. The remainder has been smoothed and rounded off by the action of the water.[1]

The Islet's resemblance to a bald pate was heightened by the light brown colour of the diabase, especially since it turned black underwater. However the name Skull Rock appeared only after the mine closed. The vein Brown brought to Macfarlane's attention that day cut the Islet transversely, near the centre, and contained "calcspar with galena and blende."

On July 10, a Friday, the party returned to Island No. 4 prepared to blast out a sample of galena, known today as sphalerite. One man held the drill while two others hammered it until the hole was big enough to hold black powder for blasting. A shout warned that the fuse had been lit and the men scattered for safety. Evidently John Morgan headed west. It was here, at the water's edge, that he spotted "the first nuggets of metallic silver".

Out came the hammers and drill again. According to Macfarlane's report:

A single blast was sufficient to detach all the vein rock carrying ore above the surface of the water, but further out large black patches could be observed in the vein under water, some of them, with a greenish tinge. On detaching and fishing up pieces of these they were found to consist of galena, with which were intermixed spots of an oxidized black mineral, here and there tinged with green. This black substance I succeeded in reducing on charcoal, before the blowpipe, with a little borax, to metallic silver, thus exposing at once the extraordinary richness of the vein.[2]

The exciting saga of Silver Islet Mine was about to begin.

Underwater the vein showed up as startling white lines which contrasted with the dark diabase of the dike. Morgan's rich vein joined with Brown's just offshore and continued in a northwesterly direction toward the mainland. A search for it there on Saturday proved to be time-consuming and fruitless. Sunday always being observed as a day of rest, Macfarlane sent them all back to Island No. 4 first thing Monday morning with instructions to break the ore loose with crowbars if necessary. That afternoon they succeeded, somehow, in setting off another blast.

Macfarlane reached Fort William on Wednesday, his boat carrying two packages of the best ore and a single piece weighing 500 pounds. Hogan and the Brown brothers unloaded the three parcels, then rowed to Thunder Bay Mine to have their tools sharpened. The following morning at daybreak, just as they spotted the *Algoma* rounding Thunder Cape, the men set out for Camp Bay.

The *Algoma* dwarfed the little boat as it passed by. The sidewheeler carried an excursion party of some 140 people representing the Press Association of Canada. The trip offered members and their wives a cruise up the Great Lakes from Collingwood, as well as an opportunity to send to their hometown papers firsthand information about Ontario's frontier mining region.

The Association released a diary account of the trip in a newspaper called *The Canadian Press*, suitable for reprinting. The entry for July 16 noted that a stamp mill lay in pieces on the dock at Thunder Bay Mine, that their ship had to anchor offshore "where the road to Fort Garry commences" (the future site of Port Arthur), that an eight-gun salute signalled their arrival within sight of Fort William, and even that the group witnessed the spectacle of an evening thunderstorm on Thunder Bay.[3]

What a story they missed! Accompanying them on the return journey were three heavy packages addressed to A. Handyside, Secretary, Montreal Mining Company.

CHAPTER 4

ALL HANDS TO SILVER ISLET

Handyside and the directors listened attentively to Macfarlane's glowing report that winter, back in Montreal. "I've named it Silver Islet," he told them, adding a strong recommendation to develop the property as a mine. The site had several advantages. The strait between Burnt Island and the mainland offered a 20- to 30-foot draft for shipping and there was enough flat ground for a mill conveniently located beside a stream.

The ore assayed at more than 5 percent silver so that the 1,336 pounds he'd forwarded were worth $1,200.[1] Experts from Toronto and Boston confirmed the richness of the find.

This amount wouldn't cover the company's total outlay, but it certainly helped defray the cost of the expedition. The directors voted to develop the Woods Location, but for sale. They renewed Macfarlane's contract, instructing that he complete his geological survey, improve the property and extract as much ore as possible.

1868 had been a banner year for the Thunder Bay region. Inauguration of regular steamship service from Collingwood had attracted visitors and tourists as well as workers for the mines and for building the overland route westward. The growing traffic warranted a contract between the steamer *Algoma* and a Bruce Mines firm to supply cordwood to fuel its boilers for the return trip. Thomas Marks & Bro. sent an agent to Thunder Bay in 1868 to build a dock for loading the wood. He soon began selling groceries, clothing and tools from a scow tied alongside. And on the shore James Flaherty catered to public demand by building a "Tavern Tent Hotel". The place began to look like a frontier boomtown.

The mining boom extended to Nipigon Bay as well. The new Hudson's Bay Company post manager there complained bitterly about its effect on business:

What with mineralogy, geology, etymology, syntax and prosidy veins, shafts, nuggets, lump mass & veins, lead indications, mica specimens, fire and earth and water I did not know where in all the world I had got to.

I am thinking of sending down a few iron spoons we have here to see if the eternal chattering won't turn them into silver. Who could get any information about the paltry fur trade[?][2]

Small wonder the Geological Survey decided to explore the northwest shore during the summer of 1869!

Macfarlane had supervised a similar exploration for the Geological Survey four years earlier, one that covered the northeast shore. No doubt he felt mixed emotions about the 1869 expedition under Logan's young protégé Robert Bell.

Nevertheless he approached his task for the Montreal Mining Company with customary vigour and determination. Accompanying him were John Morgan and Campbell Brown of the original crew, along with Lewis Brown, Edwin Kent, S. Poulin and a blacksmith named Olaf Grenberg. Since MacNaughton's corner post of 1846 could not be located, he arranged for Hugh Wilson of Mount Forest, Ontario to conduct another survey to confirm the Location's boundaries.

Unlike the previous year, 1869 was very stormy. Logan had calculated Lake Superior's water temperature as rising no higher than 38 decrees Fahrenheit (3 degrees Celsius) under the most favorable conditions. On Silver Islet, which took the full brunt of all winds except the northerlies, the air was often cold as well because summer breezes were less balmy after passing over the cold lake. Burnt Island protected the mainland from the wind and here the party pitched their camp.

On windy days the men performed tasks like examining Burnt Island and Shangoina Island for the northeast-trending veins marked on Wilkinson's map. No silver. They also followed the Silver Islet vein northwest across Burnt Island where it lay buried under topsoil and for a mile inland. Still no silver. Like it or not, the paylode was pinpointed in a very difficult maritime location.

Whenever weather allowed, Macfarlane ordered all hands to Silver Islet. The special cartridges he'd brought for underwater blasting didn't work. Neither did homemade fuses of cotton and pitch. He saw only one alternative:

> All hands, myself first, then took to the water up to the hips with crowbars, trying to loosen pieces of the vein. The same work continued in the afternoon, but the water being ice cold, probably not more than two yours continuous work was done in the water all day.[3]

Sometimes, during periods of "too much sea from the east", they worked from a boat using anchors and a staging of logs; the rest of the time was spent blasting on several small veins, or feeders, above the water line. Seven days on the Islet produced 3,429 pounds of silver ore to bring to Fort William for shipment.

On orders from head office Macfarlane next moved the party to Jarvis Island, all except John Morgan who remained on Woods Location. These offshore islands running southwest from Silver Islet appeared more promising than ever following Peter McKellar's recent silver find on nearby McKellar Island. Before leaving Fort William, Macfarlane contracted with a man named Merrill to supply enough timber for the buildings and structures he'd need to work the Silver Islet vein.

After a six-week absence, Macfarlane returned on August 12 to order a shaft sunk in the very centre of Silver Islet, planning to crosscut to the vein later. Macfarlane's party carried out blasting, then he hired two miners, Phillip Crebot and a Mr. Proulx. In five weeks the shaft reached a depth of 13½ feet. Macfarlane did a cost analysis of the work done so far:

> In sinking the last fathom [six feet] 50 days work consumed say at $1.50 - $75.00, add for materials 2 kegs powder $10.00, fuse, etc. say $5.00 - $90.00 per fathom.[4]

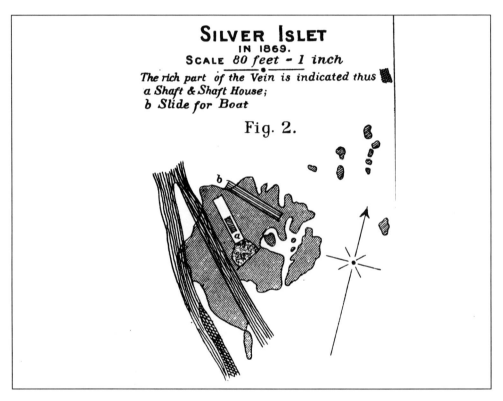

Actual construction of facilities began at the end of August, when Merrill's crew floated logs to the Islet for hewing into cribs and mine timbers. The men, all French-Canadians – Bélanger, Lacroix, Philliboth, J. Poulin, Louis Poulin, and Surprenant – lived nearby in a logging camp.[5]

Both Merrill's camp and Macfarlane's were supplied from Fort William by the Hudson's Bay Company schooner *Jessie*. That fall the *Jessie* arrived with building supplies such as bricks and lime (lime made mortar when mixed with beach sand) as well as groceries.

By the time Macfarlane left for Montreal at the end of October, the shaft and its ladders were protected by a sturdy collar of timbers. A shafthouse, which also included space for sleeping and eating, sat astride the shaft supported by a rock-filled crib.

A screen of 2-inch planks extended from the peak of the roof to the ground, to ward off the prevailing waves from the south. "At such times", Macfarlane recalled later, "we felt perfectly secure upon the islet, although from the heavy sea it was unapproachable by a boat."

The expedition had two boats. Two temporary wharves had been built on the mainland and a boat slide on the Islet itself. One night a westerly gale sent showers of heavy spray onto the screen of planks. Less than a week later a far wilder storm sent waves crashing right over the shafthouse and flooded the shaft. The next day the men found out that a 17-foot shaft holds 132 tubs full of water. It took three hours to bail it out using a makeshift windlass, a cable wound around a drum.

Macfarlane also had a boardinghouse erected on the mainland, snug enough for winter. The building was far from finished – no doors, windows or partitions – when he moved in September 7. But the day dawned so cold and wet with a biting east wind that he found the uncompleted shell "much more comfortable" than a tent. Despite these primitive living conditions, he recorded only a single sick day, taken by a miner, Mr. Proulx, who left soon afterward.

The only accident happened during construction, when Edwin Kent suffered "a severe cut with an axe on the foot". The next day Macfarlane recorded grumpily, "Kent still disabled". Three days later the injured man put in a full day's work.

Macfarlane with six men plus the two miners, and Merrill with six men, 16 in all, accomplished a great deal in two months. In addition to all their construction work, they pried loose $6,751 worth of silver ore. It was shipped to Montreal in three parcels averaging 2.76 percent, 4.344 percent and 5.147 percent silver, respectively.

Macfarlane himself didn't experience theft of minerals. However he took part in the unsuccessful search for "washed silver" stolen from Thunder Bay Mine. Peter McKellar suspected that smugglers took it to the United States:

> One party left the mine in the middle of the night, crossing Lake Superior in a small boat to Portage Lake [near Houghton] who were said by reliable persons to have brought six or seven kegs of washed silver, which could not have come from any other place at that time.[6]

The ore had been processed by the mine's new stamp mill and stored in barrels. It represented the first silver ore ever milled in Canada.

CHAPTER 5

FISHING THROUGH THE ICE FOR ORE

Macfarlane left John Morgan in charge for the winter of 1869-70. His instructions were to continue sinking the shaft, to extract as much ore as possible from the vein and to help Merrill's crew cut timber – in that order. Sharing the boardinghouse with Morgan were the cook, M. Biggar, Edwin Kent (his wound healed), Lewis Brown and S. Poulin. Add to this number Mr. Merrill and his camp of six loggers, and the total population of the nascent mining town stood at a dozen people.

Robert Bell named it Ryanton on the Geological Survey's official map, an obvious reference to the Montreal Mining Company president, Thomas Ryan. The only founding member still involved with the company, Ryan at 65 cut a commanding, even formidable, figure. Behind him lay a successful business career as a partner in the mercantile firm of Ryan Bros. & Co. of Quebec City and Montreal. His commercial links with England included acting as agent for Baring Brothers of London, the large banking and investment concern. R. G. Dun & Co. described him as "inclined in his bus[iness] intercourse to be opinionative and overbearing."[1]

Ryan was in a tight spot in 1869. Added to the company's operating cost was the new annual land tax legislated by the Ontario government. At two cents an acre the company's 18 locations – 107,098 acres – represented a drain amounting to more than $2,000 a year. The directors were in no mood to send good money after bad. When Macfarlane recommended spending an additional $50,000 developing Silver Islet as a mine, they voted against it.

Imagine the tense drama that took place in the boardroom that day, Macfarlane knowing he'd stumbled on the career opportunity of a lifetime and Ryan more determined than ever to cut his losses by liquidating the company. To Ryan, by now a vice president of the Bank of Montreal and a Senator in the new Parliament of Canada, the Montreal Mining Company and its lack of success had become a personal embarrassment.

What's more, Macfarlane had rubbed salt in the wound earlier that year. After delivering his scholarly treatise titled "On the Geology and Silver Ore of Woods Location, Thunder Cape, Lake Superior" to the Natural History Society of Montreal, he allowed it to be published in *The Canadian Naturalist*. The final paragraph stated, quite unnecessarily, that the company's money had been "injudiciously expended" at Bruce Mines.

The company displayed Silver Islet ore in England, then in September and October 1869 ordered 8,500 pounds of it smelted at Swansea, Wales. These transactions proved unsatisfactory. They realized less than $300 worth of silver to the ton even though Macfarlane valued the ore at six times that amount. Receiving no explanation for the difference, he sought an alternate smelter.

In February 1870 he forwarded almost 2,000 pounds of ore to the Newark, New Jersey firm of Balbach & Son. The processing "resulted very satisfactorily" according to Macfarlane, who valued it at more than $2,000 worth of silver to the ton. These shipments, and a parcel of 127 pounds to New York, comprised virtually all the silver ore taken out so far.

Meanwhile, back at the Woods Location, the scene was being set for 17,669 pounds of silver ore to be extracted, almost twice as much as had been pried loose in summers past. The lake around Silver Islet remained calm long enough for ice to form. As soon as he dared, Morgan ordered the men onto the ice to cut a 30-foot channel along the vein. Biggar the cook displayed his versatility by perfecting cartridges that fired underwater. Long-handled tongs and shovels were constructed on the spot. Within two weeks the ore had been lifted out and hauled to the mainland by sleigh. Macfarlane valued it at $2,070.45 per ton, or $5\frac{1}{2}$ percent silver, for a total of $18,291.39.

Table 1.
Yield in dollars 1868–1870
(Macfarlane)

The following is a statement of the entire amount of ore produced during the operations of the Montreal Mining Company, with my assays and estimates of the value of the Silver it contained:

When produced.	Net weight lbs.	Percentage of silver.	Ounces per ton of 2240 lbs.	Value per ton of 2240 lbs.	Total value.
1868	1,336	5,169	1,690	$2,095.00	$1,249.51
1869	3,429	2,760	889	1,111.25	1,701.10
1869	4,080	4,344	1,417	1,771.25	3,226.20
			Of 2000 lbs.	Of 2000 lbs.	
1869	1,946	5,147	1,680	2,100.00	1,824.37
1870	17,669	5,503	1,605	2,070.45	18,291.39
	28,460				$26,292.57

The above ore, after being sold or smelted, realized the following quantities of silver:

When sold or smelted.	Where sold or smelted.	Net weight, lbs.	Ounces per ton of 2240 lbs.	Value per ton of 2240 lbs.	Total value.
Sept. 4th, 1869	Swansea	1,209	1,397	$363\frac{1}{5}$	$962.13
Sept. 4th, 1869	New York	127			190.50
Sept. 4th, 1869	Swansea	3,322	982	$254\frac{7}{11}$	1,821.96
Oct. 29th, 1869	Swansea	4,000	880	$228\frac{1}{4}$	1,970.03
			Of 2000 lbs.	Of 2000 lbs.	
Feb. 24th, 1870	Newark, N.J.	1, 913	$1,608\frac{1}{2}$	2,075	1,984.73
Feb. 24th, 1870	Newark, N.J.	2			11.28
Feb. 16th, 1872	Newark, N.J.	17,481	1,429	1,843.41	16,112.32
Feb. 16th, 1872	Newark, N.J.	$13\frac{3}{8}$			62.40
		28, 073$\frac{3}{8}$			$28,115.35

The news hit the Montreal press in June. It made quite an impression in both England and the United States, according to Macfarlane. Only the previous month a Montreal stockbroker named E. A. Prentice agreed to purchase all the company's locations for $225,000. He'd paid $2,000 down; the first instalment of $48,000 was due September 1. The announcement amounted to free advertising for him.

He needed all the help he could get. Investor apathy seemed widespread in England. Even Ryan, with his powerful London connections, had been unable to interest investors in "distant mining enterprises". A joint offer in the United States, to A. H. Sibley and W. B. Frue, had also fallen through.

That summer Prentice partially succeeded in negotiating a sale in England on the terms of his bond – that is for a total of $225,000 in payments of $50,000 on September 1, January 1, and July 1, and $75,000 September 1, 1871. Just before the 1870 deadline the English parties telegraphed Sibley in New York offering him half interest if he assumed half the payments. Sibley agreed. But when he arrived in Montreal to transfer the $25,000, he found that they'd withdrawn altogether. Now he had to come up with another $25,000, and in a very short time.[2]

Passersby speculate on the folly of constructing mine buildings on Silver Islet, 1870.

His success marked an important turning in the Silver Islet story, the transition from the early exploration phase to full blown development as a mine. It was one of two decisions made in eastern Canada in 1870 that had a significant effect on the Thunder Bay area. The other was the military expedition under Colonel Garnet Wolseley on its way to Manitoba in the wake of Louis Riel's seizure of power at Red River.

The expedition overshadowed all other events on Lake Superior that spring and summer. Simon J. Dawson, the government engineer in charge of the overland route from Lake Superior, had collared every available man and horse to help push the road 47 miles to Shebandowan Lake. He also travelled east to arrange for boat transportation and for voyageurs, returning aboard the *Chicora*.

It was the fastest ship on the lake, this double-stacked steamer. Early on May 25 she pulled in at Silver Islet to let off some miners, then continued on to the overland starting point with Colonel Wolseley, his advance party of troops and Dawson.

That very day Wolseley named the landing site Prince Arthur's Landing in honour of Queen Victoria's 19-year-old son who'd wintered in Montreal. Prince Arthur, later Duke of Connaught, was a member of the 60th Royal Rifles, to which regiment Wolseley's battalion belonged. The settlement later became Port Arthur.

The scene was a desolate one. Less than a week before Wolseley's arrival a bushfire had swept eastward along the lakeshore. Fort William remained unscathed but the few structures at Prince Arthur's Landing had been saved only with difficulty.

Further along, the buildings at both Shuniah Mine and Thunder Bay Mine had been destroyed. At the latter, miners' wives and 18 children barely escaped with their lives by taking refuge in the mine.[3]

One event that escaped notice was William Bell Frue's guided tour of the Woods Location by Thomas Macfarlane. Frue lived near Houghton, Michigan, an Irish immigrant whose reputation rested on his experience as a mining captain in copper country.

Any link with the United States Irish was dangerous in 1870, a year of increased Fenian raids on Canadian territory. Wolseley considered the threat serious enough to mount guns at Prince Arthur's Landing "of sufficient strength to hold out against any number of Fenians that could possibly be brought against it".[4] The Fenians never came, but a different kind of invasion was already in the making.

Silver Islet's mining potential impressed Frue. He recommended that Sibley go ahead with the purchase, and asked for a bonus of $25,000 if the mine's net profit within one year should exceed a quarter of a million dollars.[5] This amount covered the purchase price plus the bonus. Sibley sent a telegram of confirmation from Montreal. When the transfer took place September 1, Frue was already at Silver Islet with manpower and materials.

His arrival came as a complete surprise to Macfarlane. "The first intimation which I had of the sale of the whole property was at Silver Islet", he admitted later, "on the night of the 31st of August, when the propeller 'City of Detroit' arrived."

William Bell Frue (1830–1881)
worked as superintendent from 1870 to 1875,
bringing Silver Islet into production.

WILLIAM BELL FRUE (1830-1881)

William Bell Frue won fame and fortune during the five years he supervised operations at Silver Islet Mine, and deservedly so. He was an engineer, inventor, speculator, manager, politician and negotiator all rolled into one. The challenges he overcame have captured imaginations for more than a century.

The task called for a daring and knowledgeable mining engineer, therefore a good deal of credit must go to the experience he gained in the copper mines around Portage Lake, Michigan.

Frue arrived in Michigan's Keweenaw Peninsula in 1853 at age 23. He had grown up in County Down, Ireland, and lived in northern New York state for a time before heading west to seek his fortune.

Little is known about his education and training except that his letters mirror an impressive level of competence in the English language and in business. His correspondence written while at Silver Islet mine survives, as well as an article about the mine's development printed in the *Annual Report* for 1873. As for mining activities in Michigan, only vague references to a Frue shaft and to his discovery of the South Pewabic mine have been found.

After his marriage to Helen Lucretia Adams, he built an imposing home directly across from the Portage and Grand Portage Mines, in what is now Houghton. The couple's first son died in 1864, and he is buried in a private cemetery near the house.

A niece from Hancock recalls him as a "raw boned fellow who did not always meet the specifications of what the artist might classify as handsome." A stranger described him as "a quiet, modest mining man of craggy, rugged appearance, dark red wiry hair and whiskers." Certainly his photograph suggests a person with a strong and determined personality and this is borne out by his actions.

He dominated the scene at Silver Islet for five years, from 1870 to 1875, then returned for a visit in September of 1876. The following summer he brought his children to Silver Islet, perhaps to see their early home.

This home became known as "Burry Worry" when Silver Islet developed as a summer community. One cold winter day in March 1930 the structure burned to the ground. The owners, Mr. and Mrs. F. R. Hobson, reported a century-old table and an oak cabinet, as well as photographs, letters and papers, as among the items lost.

In 1872 Frue had written to an investor that "Silver Islet will be a paying mine long after you and I are mouldering in our graves." He was right in that he died three years before the mine closed.

Frue had moved to Detroit after the death of his friend A. H. Sibley in 1878. He died there early in 1881 at the age of 51, and is buried in Woodlawn Cemetery.

CHAPTER 6
FIFTY-EIGHT IMMIGRANTS

Frue tackled the exploitation of Silver Islet as if it were a military campaign. Like Wolseley, he brought advance troops with him. Most of the men aboard the *City of Detroit* were mining veterans of the copper country around Portage Lake, the area served by Houghton. They'd been born in New England and Quebec, in Europe – Cornwall, Ireland, Germany – and in Michigan.

There was Frue's brother-in-law, John C. Hodgson, who was the mining captain, and his assistant, David Hodgson. Supervising construction of the physical plant were William T. Forster, mechanical engineer, and Charles H. Palmer, civil engineer. Clare Palmer was in charge of supplies, assisted by Conrad Kalb, while W. R. Noble kept the books and did the payroll.

There was the surface captain Frank Grison,* pitman James Downey, and 13 miners – Patrick Flavin, James Hanlin,* Daniel Harrington, John Harrington, Duncan Laurie, Dennie Leary, William O'Brien, Edward O'Neil, John Simmons, Tim Smith, J. T. Sullivan, Paul Sullivan, and Robert Welch.* Timberman William Purcell was experienced in timbering mineshafts and associated structures. Joseph Ames was general surface boss. Jeremiah and Josiah Gilbert worked respectively as timberman and engine driver, and John Jilbert was the blacksmith.[1]

Frue not only imported people and expertise across Lake Superior, he also transferred a way of life that had taken a quarter century to develop in Michigan's copper country. Most minetowns there were located at least 20 miles from the nearest supply centre and companies were accustomed to providing such essentials as housing and medical care.[2]

That's how Dr. Myron Tompkins came to accompany the group, also chief carpenter Chris Schuyler and his assistants Charles Bomback and George Riddle, and a couple to run the boardinghouse, Mr. and Mrs. Robert Down.

Elizabeth Down was not the first woman to work at Silver Islet Landing. When it was Ryanton, Macfarlane hired Mary Anne Pishke as cook in order to release Mr. Biggar for other duties. The woman worked for three days in the unfinished shell of a boardinghouse. On the fourth day Macfarlane recorded, without explanation, that "Pierre Pishke and wife left."

He'd hired Jane McPherson as cook in the summer of 1870, and her husband,

* Alternate spelling for Grison is Gleeson, for Hanlin is Hanley, for Welch is Walsh.

Alex, as butcher. Scottish immigrants, the couple had lived at Bruce Mines before moving to Fort William in 1868. Alex and Jane McPherson arrived at Silver Islet with three children, John, Ann and baby Mary. The family formed the nucleus of a Presbyterian congregation, sufficient to warrant Silver Islet being one of a three-point charge under student minister Vincent that summer.

The McPhersons stayed on under the new management. Unfortunately, both daughters soon died of dysentery despite Dr. Tompkins' best efforts. In October 1870 Ann McPherson, age 3, became the first person to be buried in Silver Islet's cemetery. Mary McPherson, age 7 months, followed in November.

The McPhersons and the Downs were kept busy feeding three dozen men and more in cramped quarters. The men who disembarked from the *City of Detroit* with their personal luggage set to work unloading the ship and unhitching the scow and logs it had towed across the lake. Freight included lumber, stoves, foodstuffs and tools. A scow loaded with machinery and a hoist was moored to Macfarlane's little wharves, along with a raft of some 20,000 square feet in large-sized timber.

Mining took first priority.[3] Working 18 hours a day the men bolted logs together to form a crib for a breakwater. A month later, under the supervision of civil engineer Palmer, cribbing 460 feet long and 13 feet wide had been placed alongside the Islet and filled with rocks from the mainland. Inside this breakwater a coffer dam was being constructed to enclose 70 feet along the vein. Three hundred tons of clay and other materials had been shipped from Detroit for its construction. Upon completion, it was pumped dry with steam siphons.

Frue ordered mining begun within the coffer dam as an open pit operation. Between October 5 and close of navigation a total of 155,543 pounds of ore had been extracted and shipped for processing to Balbach & Son in New Jersey.

Silver ore is a far more complex mineral than copper. Fortunately for Frue, Macfarlane agreed to stay on to superintend the assaying of the ore. He valued it at $1,205.44 a ton for a total of $93,748.99; Balbach's assay was very close at $91,445.16. It seemed as though Frue was already well on the way to collecting his bonus, despite a severe storm that halted mining for more than three weeks. There were four major storms that fall and winter.

The southeasterly gale that hit Silver Islet October 26 damaged the works extensively. Almost half the breakwater was taken out and the coffer dam damaged. Rocks spilled into the lake and also into the open pit through breaks in the coffer dam. Palmer decided to double the width of the cribbing to 26 feet. Cleanup began at once.

Repairs were well under way on November 6, a Sunday, when the first of the miners' families arrived. The *Algoma* steamed around Burnt Island to let off Rev. Joseph Hodgson, a Methodist minister, and 24 women and children. What a joyous reunion took place! And of course the day did not end without a religious service.

Arriving for the winter was Helen Adams, wife of William B. Frue, along with Nellie, age 4, Grace, age 3, and baby Willie; also her sister, Abigail, wife of John C. Hodgson, and children; Nancy, wife of Dr. Tompkins, with two children; Mrs.

Frank Grison and children; Marguerite, wife of James Hanlin, and children; and Mrs. William T. Forster with three children, accompanied by Miss Anna M. Forster.

One wonders whether houses awaited these six wives, or whether they lived in tents or a single large building at first. The records show almost $80,000 being spent, including "making provision for wintering", but no details are given. As many as eight more wives arrived with their children before the close of navigation.

Mine families, then as now, were accustomed to roughing it during development of a mine. That is not to say they didn't look forward to better living and working conditions, just that they were willing to wait. Despite the limited expectations, that first winter at Silver Islet provided what Frue called "a severe lesson" in terms of local weather conditions.

The previous year the ice had formed quickly and acted as a bridge between the Islet and the mainland for Macfarlane's men. Then in spring it softened gradually and drifted away.

The season of 1870-71 proved to be very different. The ice broke up soon after it froze and chunks of it floated back and forth all winter, driven by the wind and currents. Travelling to the Islet by boat was hazardous indeed, but it was the only means of access. "Icebergs" three feet thick and as much as 50 feet square had to be pushed aside to allow a boat to pass.

A big blow before Christmas tore out enough cribbing to spill 3,000 tons of rock into the lake and covered everything above water with a slippery film of ice. Undaunted, Frue offered a reward to anyone who found a stand of timber to repair the damage, since both the supply he'd brought from Houghton and the 30,000 feet cut on site were almost exhausted. A grove of Norway pine "on the northwest slope of Thunder Cape mountain" amply filled the need, and repairs were made.

An even bigger blow came on March 8. The wind roared and whistled relentlessly across the lake, sending tons of sharp-edged ice crashing into the breakwater. Along the entire length of the cribwork logs splintered and broke, leaving only tufts of slivers at the ends. Many of the two-inch-thick metal bolts snapped, or twisted. One observer growled, "They might as well have been my wife's hair-pins!"

The storms that battered the breakwater during the rest of the month of March spilled 6,000 tons of rock into the lake and destroyed 50,000 feet of timber. Frue compared the assault to a sustained military siege: "It seemed as though the water would surely succeed in regaining the whole of its territory and in driving its invaders from the ground."

Luckily the coffer dam remained firm, even though angry waves dashing over the top flooded the pit in no time. It was clear that Frue would have to draw up a better line of defence, one strong enough to withstand the awesome power of Lake Superior in all its moods. Time was short. In order to win his bonus, he had to extract enough silver ore to make up a quarter of a million dollars before September 1, 1871.

CHAPTER 7

EARNING FRUE A BONUS

The new breakwater faced southeast, the direction of the most violent gales. It measured 75 feet wide at the base, and was timbered in five bulkheads, with the outer one 18 feet high and facing the lake at a 45 degree angle. This and other cribwork held 50,000 tons of rock.

Frue had two large scows for carrying heavy loads to the Islet and two steam tugs to tow them, the *Ed. Gallagher* and the *Helen Grace*. He usually assigned tasks like ferrying passengers and running errands to a more elegant workhorse, the steam yacht *Silver Spray*.

There were never more than 20 miners working in the open pit at any one time. Still, the operation employed at least 150 other workers, more if Frue could get them, during the busy summer of 1871. On the mainland, new build-

The steam propeller Silver Spray, seen here at Silver Islet Landing, measured 16 feet wide and 75 feet long. She was built in 1869 by the Carroll Brothers of Sandusky, Ohio, and owned by Silver Islet Mine 1872–1883.

ings had to be constructed and existing ones upgraded – dwellings and boardinghouses as well as warehouses and a company store. other facilities had to be provided too, such as wharves and mooring space for the company's fleet and for commercial steamships making deliveries and pickups.

On the Islet Frue focused attention not only on the new breakwater but also on protecting the vein itself. On May 1 the open pit measured 8 x 65 feet at the surface, with a depth of 32 feet. By July, when miners had blasted out another 18 feet, a watertight, aboveground shaft of heavy timbers had been installed complete with an air shaft and a working shaft. At this point the space around the shaft timbers was entirely filled in with stone and hydraulic cement, right to the inside wall of the coffer dam. From now on Silver Islet mine was an underground operation.

New construction included a shafthouse, enginehouse for equipment to run the hoist and pumps, and a rockhouse for sorting the ore. Range lights were installed on some of the buildings as navigation aids. Incorporated into the cribbing were ramps for unloading and loading the scows and slips for mooring the tugs.

All this activity attracted attention, much more than the previous year. The *Toronto Globe* seemed undecided whether to put Silver Islet in its "Canada" or "United States" columns, but had no doubts about including production numbers and figures. A news item in the June 9 issue, headlined "Silver Mines and Lake Superior", is typical:

> The steamer "Chicora", on her last trip from Thunder Bay, brought down $15,000 worth of ore, which was obtained from Silver Islet, Thunder Bay. One large piece alone was valued at $4,000. The mining company have at present 480 men employed at the Islet, and have in project to crib in four acres around the ledge, which is now covered by the waters of the lake.

Silver Islet Landing became a regular port of call that summer of 1871. The new sidewheeler *Manitoba*, for example, included Silver Islet in advertising a grand excursion from Toronto "to Fort William and intermediate ports". The trip cost $30 return.[1]

Both the *Chicora* and the *Manitoba* carried the Royal Mail to Silver Islet, although no postmaster had been appointed. Lake Superior shipping linked all points along its coastline, whether in Canada or the United States. And the distance from Silver Islet to Fort William was about the same as to Isle Royale; to Duluth even shorter than to Sault Ste. Marie. Frue himself, like the *Globe*, seemed confused about jurisdiction. In June he placed an order with A. H. Sibley for United States postage stamps in denominations of 48, 24, 12, 6, 3, 2 and 1 cents.

Sibley had visited the previous fall to familiarize himself with his new holdings. In July and August he supervised exploration of Jarvis Island. The subsequent sale of the Jarvis Location to an English firm and to Simon Mandelbaum of Detroit netted the company a cool $150,000.

Even so, production at Silver Islet mine proved more profitable than the Jarvis sale. By the close of navigation in November 1871, almost $650,000 worth of silver had been extracted. Add to this the $90,000 or so from the previous fall and the total comes close to three quarters of a million dollars, three times more than Frue needed to win his bonus.[2]

More important for the future, the breakwater survived the dreaded south-easterly gales that swept across the lake. Granted the winds didn't reach the force of the previous fall. Still, during the last week in October Frue wrote about workmen on the centre line of cribwork being "tossed about like nut shells".

The sea rolled up and picked five of them up at ease, throwing them up on top of the lumber pile, which is 14 feet above the level of the lake and forty feet from the front line of cribwork.[3]

Only a single line of cribwork protected the shore side, facing Burnt Island. Here, beside the slips, carpenters were busy placing windows in a new, two-story boardinghouse, readying it for winter occupancy. Nothing could stop Frue now.

CHAPTER 8

CLAIMJUMPER!

Silver Islet's quick success rested firmly on the strong bond of trust that existed between Frue, the man in the field, and Alexander H. Sibley, the man at head office. Both received an annual salary of $5,000, Frue as superintendent of Silver Islet Mine and Sibley as president of the company. Both men were committed to overcoming the challenges presented by the mine.

Sibley had called a meeting of investors in New York on November 2, 1870 in order to finalize the purchase from the Montreal Mining Company. That day a deed of trust transferred title to shareholders on the basis of 1600 shares. Head office was designated as 52 Broadway, New York, and five trustees were appointed: Sibley as president, his friend Charles A. Trowbridge as secretary, major shareholder Edward Learned as treasurer, with Peleg Hall and Eber B. Ward as members at large.

One of their early decisions was to build a smelter, a response to continuing problems with conflicting assays. Not surprisingly, they hired Thomas Macfarlane as superintendent. Eber B. Ward claimed the presidency of the smelting company, so that the relationship between him and Macfarlane resembled the one between Sibley and Frue. Since Ward lived in Detroit the first sod was turned in Wyandotte, just ten miles away on the Detroit River, easily accessible to Silver Islet through the Great Lakes. The Wyandotte Smelting and Refining Works began operations July 1, 1871. By September 1, 1873 the plant had produced 931,203 ounces of fine silver.[1]

Ward spent the profits on his family:

> It was Silver Islet millions that bought for his beautiful and accomplished daughter, Miss Clara Ward, a husband and title, the Princess of Chimay, and it was the remnant of Silver Islet money that not long ago carried the Princess with her Hungarian fiddling lover, Jarezy Rigo, "from the gay world of European capitals".[2]

It was not at all unusual for rich North Americans to seek such marriages during the 1870s.

Sibley lived in Detroit too, although his mining and financial interests often took him to New York and to various minesites throughout the United States.

OFFICE OF
WYANDOTTE SILVER SMELTING AND REFINING COMPANY,

Wyandotte, _____ 187__

Opened _Sixteen_ Barrels No. 1 _____ Silver Ore, called

Lot No. _20_ , _9132_ lbs. Net, _1924.8_ ozs. per Ton.

No. of Barrel.	No. of Barrel.	No. of Barrel.	No. of Barrel.	No. of Barrel.	No. of Barrel
561	564	567	570	573	575
562	565	568	57	574	576
563	566	569	572		

Received 24 9134 lbs. net

Less ____ 2 " Samples sent to T. &.

Total ____ 9132 lbs to be smelted

WEIGHT AT WORKS.

Wyandotte Silver Smelting and Refining Works,

WYANDOTTE. *October 21* 18*73*

Received *from Silver Islet Lake Superior Ont*

By Steamer Manitoba September 16/78.

Oct 11/73.38 Barrels A#1 ore. 19133–1951=17182

"

"

No. of Barrel.	GROSS.	TARE.	NET.	No. of Barrel.	GROSS.	TARE.	NET.
1195	437	52	385	1214	414	44	370
1196	444	54	390	1215	552	52	500
1197	452	48	404	1216	436	48	388
1198	526	52	474	1217	396	47	349
1199	557	54	503	1218	524	51	473
1200	450	46	404	1219	429	47	382
1201	472	44	428	1220	524	52	472
1202	472	50	422	1221	538	54	484
1203	502	50	452	1222	454	46	408
1204	504	48	456	1223	540	50	490
1205	640	74	566	1224	475	48	427
1206	519	48	471	1225	424	42	382
1207	624	60	564	1226	508	50	458
1208	574	68	506	1227	530	49	481
1209	500	50	450	1228	530	47	483
1210	494	48	446	1229	426	50	376
1211	514	48	466	1230	464	50	414
1212	723	64	609	1231	412	46	366
1213	534	54	480	1232	619	66	553
				B/L.	19.241	1.900	17.341
				Returns	19.133	1.951	17.182
				Short			159

JCK

6

He'd been a forty-niner during the California gold rush. He also held the rank of major, a courtesy title. A son of Judge Solomon Sibley, the first mayor of Detroit, and a brother of Brigadier General Henry H. Sibley, the first governor of Minnesota, A. H. Sibley enjoyed important political and legal contacts in the United States. Imagine his surprise to find that a claimjumper almost succeeded in whisking Silver Islet from under his nose!

He first found out about the attempt on December 21, 1871, the day after the Ontario Liberals replaced the previous Conservative provincial government. It bears the marks of political patronage and legal hairsplitting. Evidently Frue knew that a legal loophole existed concerning underwater mineral rights. The previous June he'd obtained a government licence to cover 170 feet along the course of the vein as it extended into Lake Superior. But on December 19 the incumbent Attorney General, in one of his last official acts, handed down a decision to uphold the application of a Mr. Seymour of Toronto and England to purchase 400 acres at a dollar an acre:

Major A.H. Sibley (1817–1878), President of the Silver Islet Mining Company from 1870 until his death in 1878.

> The area, as shown by the plan filed with the application, embraced not only Silver Islet and the works upon it, but also the wharves and warehouses built by the Sibley syndicate on the mainland.[3]

Seymour had already paid the purchase price of $400.

Sibley promptly filed for a stay of title in order to prepare a defence. After a full description of the circumstances surrounding the purchase from the Montreal Mining Company, his report expanded on the company's activities and how they benefitted the country:

> Our expenditure in and about Silver Islet within a year has been about $200,000 exclusive of the purchase money....

> We have paid about $240,000 to Canadians for their rights and beside the money earned by the large number of Canadians to whom we give employment, we are obliged to spend money in Canada in very considerable quantities.

> During the last year we paid for supplies in Toronto about $40,000 and in Collingwood $15,000 besides paying freight and other incidentals. We have paid the Government for timber and have been taxed large sums. We are obliged to keep up an organization in Ontario which involves the expenditure of money.

> We have, by our success, caused large additions to be made in one year to the revenue of the Crown Lands Department than had been made from the same source for many years before, I believe; and what is better still for the country, we have been the direct and immediate cause of directing capital into the Lake Superior region, which had almost become a sealed country...

We have, on more than one occasion, relieved a government steamer with surveying parties on board, at great inconvenience to ourselves, with coal without which she could not have left our harbour ....

We have given a great deal of encouragement to the Indians. We employ them in large numbers and give them the same pay as we give to others...

The number of men employed on and about Silver Islet is 170 summer and 130 winter, apart from the force employed in smelting and otherwise.[4]

Sibley submitted his written statement, along with supporting documentation, to the new Commissioner of Crown Lands, W. R. Scott, who sought an opinion from the provincial Surveyor-in-Chief. That opinion favoured Sibley, and the new Cabinet concurred on June 22, 1872.

The scare prompted Sibley to extend every effort to protect his investment. On February 2l, 1872, the trustees deeded the Woods Location to a new company organized under the laws of New York state, the Silver Mining Company of Silver Islet, more commonly known as Silver Islet Mining Company. They also conveyed to it all buildings, machinery and stores on both the mainland and the Islet, as well as 60 percent ownership in the Wyandotte Smelting and Refining Works.

In Ontario, the trustees succeeded in incorporating themselves through legislation assented to March 2, 1872 called "An Act to incorporate 'The Ontario Mineral Lands Company'". This move provided a convenient umbrella for the other locations purchased from the Montreal Mining Company and also necessitated setting up a Toronto office, as already noted in Sibley's report. The financial report for 1871 and 1872 records heavy legal costs "for general expenses, including law fees and legal expenses in Canada and New York". Payments totalled $21,872.[5]

Despite the federal incorporation of the Montreal Mining Company, the new owners of its Lake Superior locations rarely turned to the federal government for assistance. Instead they contacted W. R. Scott, Ontario Commissioner of Crown Lands, and Adam Crooks, a member of the Ontario Cabinet. No doubt these provincial contacts facilitated the following transactions, all costing a dollar an acre. In July Sibley acquired a 341-acre water lot fronting the Woods Location, and another of 4,833 acres the following May. By the end of 1873 he also held title to 3,576 acres of timberlands near the location.[6]

The remarkable trust between Frue and Sibley never faltered, despite situations in which one of them made important decisions involving the other. Few would argue with Sibley's endorsement of Frue printed in the company's *Annual Report* for 1873:

Struggling against difficulties and dangers which would have appalled other men, he has never lost his heart or his head; ready to plan, prompt to execute, he has met and conquered every obstacle.

One of these obstacles was tracing the vein underwater in order to determine which water lots to buy. To meet this challenge, a complete deep sea diving outfit arrived at Silver Islet in July 1872, including helmet, weighted shoes and a life-line.[7]

Table 2.
Report of Treasurer,
December 30, 1872

REPORT OF TREASURER, DECEMBER 30, 1872

	Gold.
1870, September 19. Paid 1st instalment on purchase of the property of the Montreal Mining Company.	$50,000 00
1871, January 1st. Paid 2nd instalment on purchase of the property of the Montreal Mining Company.	50,000 00
1871, July 1st. Paid 3rd instalment on purchase of the property of the Montreal Mining Company	50,000 00
1871, September 30. paid 4th instalment on purchase of the property of the Montreal Mining Company	75,000 00
1871, September 30. Interest on above instalments to Montreal Co.	8,303 00

	Currency.
1871, September 30. Premiums on $183,363, gold, and interest on loans to pay above instalments	13,846 00
1871 and 1872.	
Paid for smelting silver ores produced from Silver Islet Mine.	60,116 11
Paid Canadian Customs on supplies and machinery purchased in United States	3,584 35
Paid Freight and insurance on ores and supplies.	36,614 12
Paid for steam tugs "Ed. Gallagher," "Helen Grace," "Silver Spray," and two large scows.	30,443 01
Paid for explorations and surveys on different locations	4,222 78
Paid for 1/3 taxes on property for 1870 (2/3 being paid by M.M. Co.).	749 22
Paid for taxes for 1871.	2,135 56
Paid for drafts of Superintendent for supplies, labor, etc. on Islet and mainland	131,662 60
Paid Premium on gold purchased to pay above drafts and interest on same.	11,284 79
Paid for mining plant, engine, and engine-house, pumps and fixtures on Islet.	7,066 04
Paid for boarding-house, office, assorting and change house on Islet.	4,651 28
Paid for breakwater, coffer-dam, and shaft on Islet/dwellings, boarding-houses, stores, warehouses, and stables on mainland.	22,325 01
Paid for teams, office furniture, bedding, etc. etc.	5,245 62
Paid for harbour, breakwater, building roads, clearing lands, etc.	14,556 11
Paid for general expenses, including law fees and legal expenses in Canada and New York	21,872 89
Paid for Wm. B. Frue, on special contract for services.	25,000 00
Paid First dividend.	166,666 66
Paid Second dividend.	96,000 00
Cash on hand	69,665 11
Total	$1,022,020 64

DR.

1870, Aug. 27.	
Amount received from shareholders to pay first instalment in gold	$50,000 00
Amount received for working capital, currency.	23,100 00
1871 and 1872.	
Sales of silver, being product of mine for 1870 and 1871	797,448 68
Sales of Jarvis Island property (6,400 acres)	150,000 00
For interest on same.	1,471 96
Total	$1,022,020 64

ASSETS.

Cash on hand	66,665 11
Atlantic Mutual Insurance Company's scrip for 1871	1,410 00
Atlantic Mutual Insurance Company's scrip for 1872	4,950 00
One half the stock and franchise of Montreal Mining Co.	
16 locations on Lake Superior, containing 94,298 acres	

Table 6.
Treasurer's Statement,
December 31, 1878

```
            TREASURER'S STATEMENT, DECEMBER 31, 1878.

Balance on hand as per report dated February 12, 1878, ..................... $27,754 19
Received from sales of silver, ........................................... 422,717 60
Received from bills payable, ...........................................  75,000 00
                                                                         $525,471 79


Paid mine agent's draft, .......................... $230,313 19
Paid for smelting, ................................  41,972 08
Paid premium on drafts drawn in gold,  .............  24,793 00
Paid surveying account, ...........................     282 86
Paid freights on ores and silver, ..................   3,328 44
Paid Insurance on ores and silver, .................  10,726 95
Paid interest,  ...................................   1,622 49
Paid office expenses, salaries, etc., ..............  11,697 06
Paid dividend No. 2, .............................   18,000 00
                                                                          513,736 07

Balance in bank, ....................................................... $11,735 72
```

REPORT OF ACCOUNTS FROM FEBRUARY 10, 1872, TO DECEMBER 31, 1873.

	Eleven Months ending Dec. 31, 1872	Twelve Months ending Dec. 31, 1873.	TOTALS	
Profit and loss, sundries.	$4,258 74	$20,240 43	$24,499 17	
Silver account for sales of silver.	344,199 56	547,556 24	891,755 80	
	$348,458 30	$567,796 67	$916,254 97	$916,254 97
General operating expenses, ...	$107,680 88	$149,024 37	$256,705 25	
Premium in currency paid on drafts drawn in gold,.	14,239 50	25,976 57	40,216 07	
Smelting, ...	23,637 24	48,603 65	72,240 89	
Freight on ore and silver, ...	4,190 66	4,008 54	8,199 20	
Insurance on ore and silver, ...	3,001 25	5,071 90	8,073 15	
Interest, ...	1,772 55	1,846 49	3,619 04	
Surveying, exploration, etc., of Company's lands, ...	1,540 64	282 86	1,823 50	
New York office:				
Expense, salaries, etc., ... $1,861 00			$9,993 67	
Stationery and printing, ... 819 83			208 95	
Telegraphs, ... 56 96			422 37	
Legal expenses, ... 7,185 00			2,020 52	
Rev. and postage stamps, ... 236 17			51 55	
$10,158 96 $12,697 06				
	10,158 96	12,697 06	22,856 02	
Dividends No. 1 and No. 2.	180,000 00	180,000 00	360,000 00	773,733 12
	$346,221 68	$427,511 44	Balance,...	$142,521 85

"BALANCE SHEET, DECEMBER 31, 1873."

ASSETS

Real Estate and Mines,	$5,774,613 12
Wyandotte Silver Smelting Works Stock,	55,500 00
Mine Equipment and Machinery,	7,066 04
Buildings Account,	79,783 98
Construction Account, Docks, Harbor, Breakwaters, etc.,	135,272 10
Tugs Account,	25,460 73
Burleigh Drill and Air Compressor,	4,510 66
New Engine and Hoisting Machinery,	31,811 96
Mine Agent, W.B. Frue, Supplies, etc.,	122,964 44
Insurance Scrip, (Atlantic Mutual Insurance Company),	7,990 00
New York Office, Furniture, Safe, Desks, etc.,	1,150 19
Cash in Bank,	11,735 72
	6,227,858 94

LIABILITIES

Capital Stock,	$6,000,000 00	
Bills Payable,	75,000 00	
Drafts of Mine Agent *in transit,*	10,337 09	
		6,085,337 09
Balance,		$142,521 85

CHAPTER 9

OF MINES AND MINING MEN

ilver Islet's success encouraged similar mining ventures and Frue became involved in most of them. During the winter of 1871-72 Thunder Bay froze over early in January. An ice road to Prince Arthur's Landing allowed a range of travel opportunities undreamed of the previous season. Frue, and others, took full advantage of the situation.

Shuniah mine reopened late in 1871 and Frue supplied 30 kegs of blasting powder to its superintendent, Captain Thomas H. Law. Around the same time a lodge of the Masonic order was founded in a bunkhouse at Shuniah Mine. Frue was accepted as a charter member and the name chosen was Shuniah Lodge. Ten other residents of Silver Islet are listed as early members.[1]

Frue also sent $932 to the Commissioner of Crown Lands to acquire mining rights on behalf of himself, McKellar and McIntyre. He travelled twice to Jack Fish Mine* near Shebandowan Lake, a gold prospect brought to his attention by Peter McKellar. Impressed by the showing there, Frue despatched Duncan Laurie with several men to test the vein. Laurie and his crew stayed 6 weeks. At the end of March they returned carrying 126 pounds of ore handpicked from the 100 tons brought to the surface. It assayed at $460 gold to the ton and $40 silver.

Frue stopped at Fort William to visit a partner in the venture, post manager John McIntyre. Both men knew full well the claim stood on land not yet covered by Indian treaty with the federal government. And both knew the province had issued a land patent for the area, known as H1, dated November 7, 1871, even though it had no jurisdiction to do so.

On March 29, two days after Frue and Laurie left the minesite, the Ojibway chief Blackstone arrived. In the words of Peter McKellar:

He ordered us all to leave until the Government would settle with the Indians, for he said if we were to stop that hundreds of white people would go right into their country and take up their land; then the Government would not settle with them.[2]

*Also called Huronian, Moss, Ardeen and Kerry.

Frue felt cheated, and blamed Simon Dawson for alerting Blackstone. He promptly wrote a letter of protest to the Ontario Commissioner of Crown Lands, then forwarded a copy to Adam Crooks, at the time Attorney General for the province, urging him "to reinstate me in my rights". He also sent a copy to the area's elected representative, F. W. Cumberland, suggesting that an investigation was in order. "I should think", Frue fumed, "that the law of the land would mete out to him [Dawson] the punishment due to those who tamper with Indians."

The same day he advised McIntyre to file a trust deed in Sibley's name. "It would be of immense interest to me if the property could be transferred two or three times considering the present state of affairs", he wrote, adding that changing ownership might strengthen the title.[3]

This is one battle Frue lost. Even after the signing of Treaty Three in 1873, undisputed title to the claim had to await settlement of a lengthy jurisdictional battle between the federal and provincial governments. As a memento of the shortlived partnership, Frue presented a "button" of the gold to McIntyre's wife, Jane.

In most other cases legal title depended upon the thoroughness of the land surveyor. Frue chose to continue with the services of Hugh Wilson, the man who ran the Woods Location's lines for Macfarlane in 1869 and who carried out the first survey of Prince Arthur's Landing in 1871.

Wilson arrived at Silver Islet March 1, 1872 in order to gather information to disprove Seymour's claimjump attempt. He made a key discovery by pinpointing Silver Islet itself, the original Island No. 4, as the base for five of the triangulations "made in 1846 and shown on field notes." Frue promptly sent Sibley a telegram, via Duluth, followed by a letter of confirmation.[4]

Never before had communication seemed so vital; never again would Frue have reason to complain so bitterly about the shortcomings of the postal service.

During navigation season, his needs were met by passenger steamers carrying the Royal Mail according to a set shipping schedule. Winter was another story. Canadian mail travelled a circuitous route through the United States via Detroit and Duluth, then every two weeks by courier to the trading post of A. A. Parker at Pigeon River, Minnesota. From here a courier under a Canadian government contract brought it to the post offices on Thunder Bay.

The system worked fairly well as long as the volume remained low enough for one man to carry. The United States courier lived in Beaver Bay, about 50 miles from Duluth and 100 miles from Pigeon River. With the increased amount of mail during the winter of 1871-72, he refused to carry it beyond Beaver Bay at the contract rate. The Canadian courier, for his part, found no mail waiting at Pigeon River and returned light.

Frue did not stand alone in his concern about non-delivery of mail. In February a local citizens' group despatched a special courier to Duluth with telegrams advising Ottawa and Washington of the situation. Within three days the Duluth postmaster received instructions to spare no expense in expediting delivery. It took four men to carry the mail that had accumulated at Beaver Bay, and several more to bring the rest from Duluth.

The special courier was Donald McKellar. His account of the journey from Fort William lends insight into the crucial role played by weather.

> We found the ice very good for travelling to Pigeon River but from there on the lake ice was floating, so we had to take to the shore, through the woods, until we arrived at Grand Marais.
>
> That night the wind turned off land and moved the ice out from the shore, leaving a clear sheet of water, permitting a rowboat to be used to good advantage. This we purchased from one of the citizens...
>
> Next morning the ice was again piled up on the shore. We had to take to the woods, and two days later arrived at Beaver Bay.

The return trip from Duluth was even worse.

> It was now near the end of February. The weather had been very cold – 20 to 30 below zero a number of times...
>
> We found the ice frozen solid enough, but in many places the great cakes of ice piled one on top of another, in every shape, so that we had to take to the bush more than we wanted to for there the snow was three or four feet deep.
>
> After a very hard tramp we arrived home safe and sound, thirty days from the time we left.[5]

Frue managed to arrange a weekly delivery between Duluth and Pigeon River, but the Canadian end of the run remained at "every two weeks". He offered to pay the courier the extra amount, and more, for weekly pickup and delivery during the month of March. However negotiations fell through when the Thunder Bay postmaster refused to deviate from biweekly service without official sanction. [6]

Summer delivery began when the first ship of the season docked at Silver Islet's mainland wharf in mid-May. Some of the mail had travelled a roundabout route, much to Frue's disgust. He acknowledged receiving plans and correspondence from surveyor Wilson. "All went by way of Duluth, Collingwood and God only knows where", was his wry comment. He promptly submitted a longterm proposal to the Canadian post office in order to assume responsibility for the winter mail himself.[7]

Frue also had to deal with charlatans like W. A. Northrup, the front man for the Otter Head tin swindle. In 1871 Northrup convinced him to invest in a north shore vein allegedly discovered by Homer Pennock and John W. Johnston. Frue arranged for $4,000 backing, that is $1,000 each for himself, Sibley and two others.[8]

On the strength of this support Northrup commissioned a survey of Homer township.* A party of some 22 men sailed to Otter Head aboard the *Manitoba* on her last trip of the season. After carrying out the survey, they arrived at Prince Arthur's Landing in mid-February, on foot, and delivered the survey papers to Northrup. Frue became suspicious when Northrup refused to visit him at Silver Islet, preferring instead to confirm their agreement by courier.

On April 4 he confided to a colleague:

> If the patents are issued I will undoubtedly have my interest although there appears now to be something like "foul play" connected with it. If they succeed they are welcome to it.[9]

The original investors, including Frue and Sibley, paid Northrup the entire amount in cash and stock, and also covered the cost of the land, at a dollar an acre, and the survey.[10]

Afterwards Frue hired Peter McKellar to check out Homer township for minerals, supplying him with "an elaborated report, with map and detailed plans, of the various deposits of tin ore."[11] McKellar found no trace of tin during six weeks on the site.

Oddly enough it was McKellar who witnessed the delivery of material to "salt" the vein, an attempt to profit on the stock as well as the original scam. Upon Pennock's insistence that the tin lay outside the area surveyed, Northrup sent a party to survey another township north of Homer.

Choice of the name Byron, the surname of one of England's greatest satirists, for the township was a nice touch. Even the weather favoured the daring crooks. In November 1873, investors sent Captain William Harris of Ontonagon to the site as an independent mining expert. He confirmed the existence of tin, but under conditions that were far from ideal: a pending storm, an impatient schooner captain, and six inches of snow on the ground.

The stock sold very well, mainly because of Harris' endorsement. McKellar himself expressed amazement at the realistic arrangement of the salted material, said to have been placed by a Mr. Childs of Duluth. But the tin originated from Cornwall. The bubble burst soon after breakup when Frue and others discovered the hoax.

Legitimate discoveries along the north shore in 1872-73 included gold and silver at Heron Bay and iron at the Little Pie River. Sibley bought into both these finds, as well as the existing Enterprise lead mine on Black Bay. The English parties backing the Jarvis Island development had only recently abandoned the Beck silver mine** as unprofitable. Frue suggested they invest in Heron Bay as an alternative.

---

* Today, Homer township has been incorporated into Pukaskwa National Park, also Byron township.

**Also called Silver Harbour and 3A.

Frue took the Jarvis Location under his wing for the new owners. He had Wilson survey its coastline as water lots, a response to the claimjumping attempt. He reported the fate of Thomas Stratton and John Pelong, two workmen who set out in an open boat and didn't make it to shore. He also had Thomas Macfarlane's successor, Walter McDermott, assay the ore.[12]

Mining continued at Jarvis Island under mining engineer John W. Plummer. Captain John, as he was called, came from Bruce Mines where he had succeeded his father, William, as superintendent. He also represented the North American interests of John Taylor & Sons of London, England. The elder Plummer had been in charge of the Northern Superintendency of the federal Indian Affairs Department since 1868.

Which of the two positions induced Peter McKellar to ask Captain John to assess the Jack Fish gold find is not known. Perhaps both of them. In any case, the young man met McIntyre's daughter, Fanny, and fell in love. The couple married at Fort William in September 1872 and moved to Silver Islet, where their first child, Daisy, was born.

At least two titled Britons visited Lake Superior's mines during 1872 with a view to investing. William Viscount Milton and Lady Milton spent the summer at Pointe de Meuron, upstream from Fort William, in a house owned by McIntyre.[13] Here Lady Milton, attended by her personal physician, gave birth to a son and heir, the seventh Earl Fitzwilliam.

During the same summer Frue escorted Earl Dunraven of Limerick, Ireland, to Ontonagon, where he owned mining properties. For the occasion Frue had ordered a large supply of bourbon and gin, as well as goblets and glasses ground with the letter "F", for delivery to his home in nearby Houghton. An avid sportsman and collector, Dunraven requested that Dr. Tompkins and Walter McDermott collect Indian relics for him.

The following year Dunraven visited Silver Islet again, this time with his wife. The couple had agreed to be godparents for two of Frue's children. The christening on August 25 was a major social event, with the Anglican minister C. B. Dundas journeying from Prince Arthur's Landing to officiate at the ceremony. Among those who attended were A. H. Sibley and his brother H. H. Sibley, along with their households.[14]

Then in August 1874 the Governor General of Canada, Lord Dufferin, arrived aboard the *Chicora*. Lady Dufferin recorded the event in a letter home:

> We went over from the mainland in a tug, and saw all that could be seen without actually going down the mine. The silver is in fern-like patterns in a sort of white quartz. The "captain" of the undertaking is a "Frew" from County Down, and talks of going home this year to put up a monument to his mother in Bangor Churchyard.[15]

The first lady had succeeded in wheedling more personal information from Frue than he usually admitted.

CHAPTER 10

AN IMAGE OF PERMANENCE

By the 1870s the streets in many minetowns looked like any residential city block of the day, except for their isolated setting. Rows of two-story detached dwellings, either log or frame, stood on generous lots often as large as 75 x 100 feet. Fences marked the lot lines and protected gardens from domestic animals grazing outside the townsite. The dirt road fronting each house linked with a main artery leading to the mine.

Silver Islet Landing differed in three respects. Company houses enjoyed a spectacular setting facing the lake; being located on a major shipping lane brought the world to its doors; and the mine, complete with squealing hoist and belching smokestack, lay outside the range of sight or sound for most residents. If minetowns were ranked on a scale of one to ten, Silver Islet Landing would rate a ten.

Like other minetowns, Silver Islet was an instant community. When Sibley defended his ownership of the mine early in 1872, he included the following statement:

> On the Woods Location, within a year, we have established a colony of about 300 souls, almost all Canadians.

This is true if the word "Canadians" is translated as British subjects. Whether employees arrived from the old country via Canada or the United States their accents usually gave them away: Tretheweys from Cornwall, Livingstones and Strachans from Scotland, Frue from Ireland. People born in Ontario, like J. W. Cross, seemed to be in the minority.

Residences in Silver Islet Landing varied in architectural style, and it was size and level of ornamentation that reflected the mine's hierarchy. The largest and most ornate homes were set apart from the rest as accommodation for white collar staff like the superintendent, accountant and doctor.

The mile-long dirt road fronting the houses became known as the Avenue. At its eastern end, along Sandy Beach*, lay six or seven grand homes. Across Sibley

---

* The earlier name for Sandy Beach was Crescent Bay; for Sibley Creek was Frue Brook.

Creek about forty dwellings marched down the Avenue in rapid succession, broken only by the Methodist Church.

The Methodist Church doubled as a school, with the steeple bell calling the faithful to church on Sundays and the children to class on weekdays. As early as March 1872 Frue mentioned that Duncan Laurie's children "attended school by the day". The following school year a Miss Richardson was named as teacher, "the worthy trustee having failed to obtain a man that would officiate both as teacher and minister."[1]

The building was nicknamed Old Glory, but the reference is to Methodist heaven rather than the United States flag. Except for Presbyterian student ministers during the summer, Methodists held the only regular Protestant services. Anglican clergymen visited only occasionally.

"The Doctor and Mrs. Tompkins have joined the church and go every Sunday night," reported Frue in November 1873, adding that accountant James C. Hill took advantage of the situation to visit Polly, their redhaired daughter, at home.

Hill came from Brooklyn. He lived along Sandy Beach in the white collar section, not far from the doctor's house.

The long finger of Burnt Island protected such harbour structures as a boardinghouse, company store and customs house. The Avenue's western extremity at Catholic Point* was anchored by St. Rose of Lima Church.

*Now called Sellers Point.

Married employees lived in a string of neat dwellings on the mainland. The Methodist church, left, doubled as a school and on the far right, at the end of Sandy Beach, is the President's mansion.

The church was built for the Jesuit Richard Baxter, who visited Silver Islet Landing soon after his arrival on Thunder Bay June 4, 1872. While Father Dominique du Ranquet acted as Superior of the Indian mission along the Kaministiquia River, Father Baxter served the area's growing white population as a sort of roving priest. He soon designated Silver Islet Landing as the jumping off point for other Lake Superior missions, including Isle Royale.

Why he named the church after the Peruvian Santa Rosa is not known. She was the first saint in the Americas, having been canonized in 1671, and this may have been the reason. But her relationship with mosquitoes offers another, more whimsical view:

> The mosquitoes agreed not to feast on Santa Rosa's blood, and Santa Rosa undertook never to swat at them. Instead, they all assembled each morning in the chapel and hummed their praise to the Lord, reappearing again at dusk to offer their thanks to the creator for having given them this day their daily blood - excepting, of course, the blood of the lady saint.[2]

Father Baxter performed the first marriage in St. Rose of Lima church May 25, 1873, when he joined together Adolphe Marcotte and Jane Précourt. In the 11 months since his arrival he had baptized nine infants at Silver Islet:

St. Rose of Lima Catholic Church anchored the west end of the Avenue. Behind it is the stamp mill.

The Jesuit Father Baxter was known as the pioneer priest of Thunder Bay. His first church was at Silver Islet Landing.

Marie Louise Ida Brouillet, Harry Aristide Chausse, Catherine Clark, James Flavin, Thomas Jilbert, Catherine Nemeshkawashk, Josephine Précourt, Martin Purcell and James Simmons. He had also married three couples; William Savard to Elizabeth Tamery Cole, age 23, Captain John Le Blue to Louise La Salle, age 14, and Ulderic Henry La Salle to Margaret Sullivan, age 16. As to funerals, he reported that "several burials took place during my absence. I never could get full details."[3]

Father Baxter had a distinctive personality. Nobody could mistake him for another priest, with his full beard, black cassock and much-worn hat.

> He carried crisscross on his shoulders numerous canvas bags and bundles ... which contained his vestments, candles, his portable altar, and the famous tin horn on which he was wont to blow a strident blast to summon the Catholics together. [4]

The company store's loading doors faced the lake for convenient warehousing. The water-filled barrels on the rooftop platform are for fire protection. One of the tugs is tied up at the dock.

At Silver Islet, a church bell donated by Frue called Catholics to mass. A widow's walk encircled the steeple for viewing the Islet through a gap cut in the trees across Burnt Island.

Another prominent structure was the company store, a massive three-story frame building with a full basement. Dockside, loading doors opened onto the lake; the retail side faced the Avenue.

John Davidson of Bruce Mines arrived as store manager in the fall of 1871, with Clare Palmer and Conrad Kalb staying on as assistants. In the spring Frue decided to bring in additional stock, including silks, plaids and prints for the tourist trade. He despatched Davidson to Toronto on a buying trip.

The store netted $9,906.64 in 1872 and 1873 combined. During this two-year period the inventory of merchandise on hand rose from about $30,000 to $45,300.

Frue insisted that profits derive from a higher markup on dry goods rather than on staples like flour, beef and pork.

Staple articles ... are sold at a price to enable the boardinghouse keepers to maintain the standard rate of board, which is $14 per month, and to keep intact the established rate of wages, which is $40 per month; or $26 per month clear of board.[5]

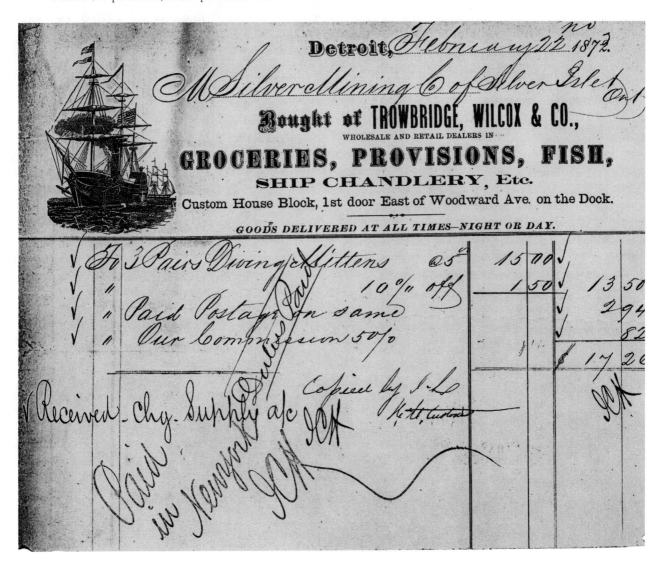

John Livingstone was Silver Islet's customs inspector and postmaster from 1872 to 1884.

This unprepossessing structure served as customs building, post office and bank for the Silver Islet community.

Each fall the store brought in enough staples to last the winter, for boarding-houses as well as single dwellings.

Across the Avenue from the store a Union Jack flew above an unpretentious frame building, announcing the presence of the government representative John Livingstone. At first customs were cleared at Sault Ste. Marie through collector Joseph Wilson. Livingstone began performing these duties as a resident sub-collector of customs soon after his appointment in June 1872.

In November he also took over as postmaster, relieving John Davidson of the responsibility. In winter, raising the Union Jack was a signal that the mail had arrived.

Livingstone, his wife, Jane, and daughters, Janey, Kate and Maude, lived in Government House, a stylish and roomy residence behind the customs house-cum-post office. The main entrance opened into the house and another door led to Livingstone's office. The family placed heavy emphasis on art, music and literature as well as manners and deportment.

Most married employees, like Livingstone, were young enough to have dependent children. Richard Trethewey arrived from the United States late in 1871 to supervise the new underground workings. He and his wife Mary Hannah brought their five little ones, aged ten and under.

The Livingstone home is fronted by a neat picket fence. The one-storey section served as an office.

James Wilmington Cross, a millwright from Owen Sound, hired on during the summer of 1871. His wife Helen Strachan accompanied two-year-old Margaret to Silver Islet Landing. In September Wilmington Alexander was born, the second of nine children.

Mrs. Cross' brother, John Strachan, began work at the same time as a miner. He continued living with the Crosses until his marriage to Catherine Stubbs. Then the couple moved into company housing and parented five children.

Although Dr. Tompkins maintained a hospital on the Islet, he handled everything else as house calls. Epidemics were especially feared in those times before immunization. Scarlet fever raged in February 1871, claiming the life of

Henry Saxton Sibley worked at Silver Islet between 1871 and 1884 as the accountant and carried on as trustee after the mine closed.

Margaret, the two-year-old child of John and Kate Simmons. The following winter typhus prevailed, an acute infectious disease spread by parasites. It may have caused the death of newborn Ketty Ann McLean in February. Unclaimed monuments for her grave were found at Silver Islet years later, still in the crate,[6] mute testimony of the uncertainty of mining as a career.

The Frues had a "lovely home with deep window ledges in French windows"[7], close to Sibley Creek. The log-and-lumber structure measured 50 x 70 feet including verandah. It had been thoroughly winterized in the fall of 1871. The following year they welcomed a new baby. "The name already selected is Argenta," Frue informed his father-in-law, "which is Latin for silver". He adored this daughter, calling her "one of the fairest little ones you have ever seen".

Choosing employees was often a family affair. That winter the Frues boarded a relative of Edward Learned, a major stockholder from Massachusetts, who worked in the company store. A member of A. H. Sibley's family, Henry Saxton Sibley, toiled as an accountant throughout the mine's life.

Everyone contributed what they could to the cultural life of the town. John Butler arrived from the United States in November 1871 to replace W. P. Noble as head accountant. In the spring he went home to fetch his wife and violin. Musical evenings became a favourite entertainment, Butler adding to the pool of musical talent in the community.

At the very end of the Avenue, overlooking the picturesque wigwams on Camp Bay, lay President Sibley's summer headquarters. The three-story frame structure faced the lake. He'd brought some furniture and cooking utensils with him in 1871, such as a walnut bedstand and porcelain pots, and also a cow to supply milk. Frue arranged a three-story addition the following year to match the existing structure,[8] in preparation for the arrival of Sibley and his wife, Maria Louise Miller.

The President's mansion served as summer headquarters for shareholders and their families.

The L-shaped building contained a carpeted apartment for the Sibleys as well as a large dining room, kitchen and any number of bedrooms. Frue assured Sibley that the White House, as it came to be called, would "be capable of accommodating any reasonable amount of visitors without the slightest interruption" in their domestic routine.

A generous porch faced the lake, its roof supported by capped wooden columns. South and east windows on the main floor eventually sported exterior shutter blinds. The entrance to the Sibley apartment featured narrow windows on each side of the door and a flower trellis along the porch.

The Sibleys had three children. The couple brought black servants with them on their visits, including a coachman. It's said that Mrs. Sibley, a classical musician, shipped her grand piano from Detroit each summer. Most guests were directors and stockholders of the mine, accompanied by their families.

Frue estimated that construction of buildings on the mainland cost the company $48,885 by the end of 1873. An additional $23,120 rendered the harbour facilities the best in the Thunder Bay region.

Table 4.
Condensed Inventory,
January 1, 1874

CONDENSED INVENTORY, JANUARY 1, 1874.		
Real estate, mineral and other lands		$5,744,613 12
MINING PLANT.		
	$ 3,500 00	
New and old hoisting engines, ...	34,741 66	38,241 66
Pumps, rods, bob, wire rope, kibbles and tools of all descriptions,		9,638 41
Engine and boiler house, boarding houses, office, shaft house, dry and changing houses,		
etc., including all buildings on Islet,		24,973 92
Breakwater, engine and house foundations, ...		112,345 54
Tugs, scows and fixtures, ...		25,350 00
		$210,549 53
BUILDINGS.		
Cost of buildings on main land, December 31, 1873, ...		48,885 44
DOCKS, HARBOR IMPROVEMENTS, ROAD & C.		
Steamboat docks, harbor breakwaters, lumber dock and dry dock, ...		23,120 44
Constructing roads and clearing land, ...		4,280 00
		$ 27,400 44
AVAILABLE ASSETS AS CAPITAL FOR WORKING MINE		
Cash on hand in office		$2,938 01
Available supplies of all kinds on hand		55,662 93
Silver ore on hand, 23.308 tons at $1,000, ...		23,154 00
Wynandotte Silver Smelting Co. stock, 2,200 shares, at $25, ...		55,500 00
Merchandise in store at landing, per inventory		43,300 42
		$182,555 36
LIABILITIES		
As per balance sheet of ledger, December 31, 1873, ...		$ 13,408 97

A tug in drydock for repairs. The long, three-storey building with altered roofline is the hotel.

The complex of cribbing and warehouses fronting the company store included docks to accommodate boats of all sizes as well as a drydock to repair company vessels. The western dock formed one breakwater and a second L-shaped breakwater on the east extended to, and formed part of, the drydock.

At the end of the dock a light 40 feet high guarded the harbour entrance, guiding ships to safety. There was only one government lighthouse in the vicinity, St. Ignace light.

Reverend George Grant was a passenger on the sidewheeler *Frances Smith* on July 21, 1872 when she pulled into the harbour shortly after midnight. His diary reflects contemporary attitudes about mining on the Ontario frontier:

> The most wonderful vein of silver in the world has been struck here. Last year, thirty men took out from it, $1,200,000... The original $50 shares now sell for $25,000...

> Such a marvellous "find" as this has stimulated search in every other direction around Lake Superior .... It would be strange indeed if all the minerals had been stumbled on at the outset. Those rocky shores are, perhaps the richest part of the whole Dominion.[9]

Grant was accompanying the government expedition led by Sandford Fleming, journeying westward to scout a suitable route for a transcontinental railway.

Shortly thereafter construction began on a modest government dock at Prince Arthur's Landing, under the supervision of Simon Dawson. This, as well as continuing surveys north of Lake Superior, mirror the expansionist policy of the federal Conservatives under John A. Macdonald. The Pacific Scandal and subsequent fall of his government late in 1873 called a halt to such activities.

Surveys at the provincial level concentrated on measuring out townships in preparation for an expected rush of settlers. In 1873 legislation created the giant Municipality of Shuniah as a basis for municipal organization. It was an unwieldy area composed of the townships ringing the northwest shore from the Canada-United States boundary to the head of Thunder Bay – Pardee, Crooks, Blake, Paipoonge, Neebing (which included Fort William), McIntyre, McGregor and McTavish – as well as the village of Prince Arthur's Landing and "the promontory of Thunder Cape with Silver Islet, and the group of islands immediately westerly thereof, to constitute and to be called the Thunder Cape Ward."[10]

CHAPTER 11
UNDER MANAGEMENT'S THUMB

T he provincial legislation that created the Municipality of Shuniah left Silver Islet in a state of limbo, but this fact went unrecognized for some time. Apparently Thunder Cape Ward could not exist as a legal entity within the terms of the Act because the Woods Location was surveyed as a mining location, not as a municipal unit such as a township or village. Sibley township, surveyed in 1874 and named for President Sibley, fell outside the limits of the Woods Location.

"An Act to Organize the Municipality of Shuniah, and to amend the Acts for establishing Municipal Institutions in unorganized districts" received assent March 29, 1873. The newly appointed stipendiary magistrate of the sub-district of Thunder Bay, Delevan D. Van Norman, had recently moved to Prince Arthur's Landing. To him fell the responsibility of arranging a smooth transition.

The Act allowed for the election of 12 councillors, one from each ward. Van Norman set the nomination date as June 16, to be followed by an election two weeks later. The polling place named for Thunder Cape Ward was the "store-house" at "Silver Islet Station", with James C. Hill as returning officer. It would be Thunder Cape Ward's first and last election for a councillor.

Frue won, but he attended only one meeting in order to take the oath of office. He had already asked Van Norman to arrange for organizing the Woods Location as a separate entity as provided under earlier legislation passed in 1872.[1] He also supplied census records and a petition to support the application, as required.

However the 1872 Act could not be applied in areas that fell within the boundaries of the Municipality of Shuniah, like the Woods Location. The Attorney General himself refused the application in a letter dated August 5, 1873.[2] In other words, the legal machinery did not exist to establish municipal government for the Silver Islet community. This oversight set a precedent by reinforcing paternalism, rather than democratic municipal government, as the ruling force in an important northern Ontario minetown.

Although taxation could not be instituted to pay for municipal services, still the community adopted some of the Act's provisions. Thunder Cape Ward participated in a municipality-wide election of school trustees on September 1, 1873, after its ineligibility was realized, in order to establish a school section. Elected as trustees to S.S. No. 3 were John Livingstone, Richard Trethewey and Lachlan McLean Morrison, a tug captain from the Isle of Mull, Scotland. A Board of Health was appointed on August 13 consisting of Frue, Dr. Tompkins and Thomas Gilmour.

The Act allowed for the appointment of a constable and establishment of a lock-up. Thomas Gilmour also acted as constable, a position closely linked to his job of searching everyone leaving the Islet. A journalist was informed in 1875 that "scarcely a day passed that one or wore attempts to smuggle away specimens were not discovered and frustrated".[3]

Silver Islet jail was built behind the stamp mill, well away from the Avenue. Sturdily constructed of squared timbers, the structure crammed five cells, a dayroom, and the jailer's office and bedroom into floor space measuring only 22 x 30 feet. Still, this arrangement was better than before, when wrongdoers had to be brought to Prince Arthur's Landing.

At first the only liquor allowed in the area was *spiritus fermenti*, whisky dispensed by Dr. Tompkins for medicinal purposes. The ban proved impractical, especially on the mainland where a supply could be had from the boats that docked there as well as from itinerant peddlers. Frue, like many of the Methodist residents, preferred temperance. He decided to stock whisky in the store and to allow each employee to buy one quart on Saturday nights.

The persistence of bootlegger lore suggests that this remedy too was flawed. Reverend Donald McKerracher visited in 1873 as the Presbyterian student minister. A staunch supporter of temperance, he was appalled by the drinking he saw. After an excursion to Black Bay on a working tug, and getting stuck on a reef, he wrote in disgust, "Whiskey is the curse of this country. Got back to Silver Islet about 3 a.m."[4] McKerracher returned the following year as an ordained minister and preached temperance throughout the area until 1880.

Frue regulated drinking on the Islet as well as on the mainland. He made arrangements that permitted one drink after each shift, or three drinks a day. On the wall behind the bar, instead of the usual gilt mirror, hung a blackboard marked off into 300 or more numbered squares. Since the numbers corresponded with an employee's payroll number, a mark in his square meant both a drink and a deduction. No man got more than his allotment.

A visitor in 1875 described the saloon as large, well lit and comfortably furnished.

> In connection with this saloon there is a very fair library, purchased by the company, and a table on which many of the leading papers and periodicals are kept for the use of the men. The bar tender acts as librarian.[5]

The five-foot-high bar was unique in that the only way to get behind it was to jump over it.

Sometimes fights broke out among the workmen, especially on Sundays.

On these occasions, Frue became very firm in enforcing order. "I give you five minutes to get off the islet to shore," he would say, "and you shall go if it takes every man on the mainland to carry you off.[6]

Silver Islet was a company town first last and always. It never functioned under an elected municipal government. Instead the company handled municipal responsibilities such as town planning, road maintenance and law enforcement. Residents' rights were limited to concessions gained through good behaviour.

CHAPTER 12

THE SINKING OF THE SHAFT

ntil 1871 the ore had been rich enough to sort by hand for shipping to the smelter. But shortly after freezeup, just about the time open pit mining changed to an underground operation, the vein began displaying sudden changes in size and richness.

The lode ... narrowed, and being at points not over six inches in width, with scarcely any packing ore in sight. During the winter it gradually widened, and produced ore in handsome quantities.

During the summer which followed [1872], the lode became broken up, being thoroughly mixed with diorite and wedges of plumbago, and in the fall the mine assumed anything but a flattering appearance.

In the following winter it suddenly changed in character, and produced, up to May 1st, 250 tons of rich packing ore, worth about $1,500 to the ton.[1]

The amount of packing ore sent to the smelter for refining, raised previously, in 1870 and 1871, was 78 tons and 486 tons respectively. In addition, a large amount of the less valuable stamp rock lay piled on the Islet.

November 1871: Depth Of Shaft 90 Feet

As soon as the mine became an underground operation in the fall of 1871, Frue required more experienced "drill and hammer" men for blasting. Before freezeup Richard Trethewey brought a select group of experienced Cornishmen to Silver Islet and remained to supervise the underground workings.

Cornish immigrants were called Cousin Jacks in Canada, as they were in the old country. The reason is unclear. Some say the nickname derived because Cornishmen always had a cousin in the old country who wanted a job. Others say the word cousin is misspelled; it should be cussin' Jacks.

In any case, individual surnames are readily recognizable through a rhyming couplet:

By Tre, Lan, Pos, Car, Pol and Pen,
You may know the most of Cornishmen.

Trethewey's Cousin Jacks spearheaded a strike that winter and halted production. Frue blamed the fact that the company paid their fare. "They get their ideas up," he raged, "and labor under the delusion that you cannot get along without them."[2] The strike ended in mid-February 1872 when eight Cornish miners left for Prince Arthur's Landing after collecting their time owing. Six of them promptly signed on at Shuniah Mine.

Coincidentally, a similar strike by Cousin Jacks closed Michigan's copper mines shortly afterward. Underground workers refused offers of a raise in pay from $60 a month to $70 in order to strike for a reduction in hours. Instead of ten-hour shifts, they wanted eight hours.[3]

One result of the strike was that Frue decided to mechanize the drill and hammer operation by applying existing technology to mining. In the summer of 1872 he brought in a Burleigh drill and air compressor costing $4,510. Its presence offered a viable alternative to established methods and reduced Frue's dependence on a commodity in short supply: experienced underground miners.

May 1872: Depth Of Shaft 130 Feet

Despite its unique underwater location, Silver Islet was considered a dry mine because of minimal seepage from its walls. However with each foot sunk, more and more water had to be pumped out further and further. Whenever the shaft flooded, inadequate pumps were always blamed. The system had to be upgraded on a regular basis.

A 40 horsepower pump on the surface sufficed at first. By December 1871 it was moved down the shaft in order to increase the draft. And on May 15 six of the miners had to carry up barrels of water on the hoist or skip.

A more powerful pump was installed shortly afterward, along with a new steam plant. So far the company had spent $7,066 for "mining plant, engine, and engine house, pumps and fixtures" including $3,500 for the original hoist still in use.

The shaft measured 8 x 14 feet, planked all the way down to make two water-tight compartments. In one of them the skip hoisted ore to the surface. The other enclosed the piping attached to the pumps as well as the ladderway from the bottom of the mine. An engine powered by steam ran both the hoist and the pumps.

The steam plant had to be manned 24 hours a day to keep the pumps operating. Ongoing maintenance and repair of the hoisting machinery, as well as "pumps, rods, bob, wire rope, kibbles and tools of all descriptions", took place on site, in the machine shop or in the blacksmith shop.

Delivery of supplies and equipment was limited to the shipping season, therefore Frue kept on hand a good supply of parts and backup equipment,

nearly double the amount needed, as regards both duplicate machinery and supplies generally, which are carefully stored away at separate points as a security against total loss by fire.[4]

The company suffered no serious fires. Precautions included sanding the buildings, covering them with mineral paint and storing water atop all large structures. Water-filled wooden barrels on fenced platforms along the roofpeaks became one of the Islet's most prominent features.

Explosives were cached in three different places, usually on islands. One of them, a small landform east of Burnt Island, became known as Powder House Rock because of the magazine there. In addition to its use underground, blasting powder was used for quarrying rock on the mainland to build the breakwater and to form a foundation for the industrial complex taking shape on and around the Islet.

Left to right are the shafthouse, rock house, engine house, smokestack and boiler house. Elevated wooden sidewalks made walking around the site easier.

November 1872: Depth Of Shaft 185 Feet

On November 12 the *Manitoba* unloaded the first shipment of a new steam-powered engine to run the hoist and pumps. Frue expressed disappointment with delays in installing it:

The weather has been very much against us for the last 3 weeks. I have not yet been able to sink a single crib for foundation of new engine - the scows having been engaged during fair weather in bringing timbers up from Black Bay. The last storm (which occurred this week) carried away about 100 tons of our rich Stamp Rock. It also picked out of the top cribwork (in South-East side) about 200 or 300 tons of rock, throwing it around the Blacksmith Shop. This crib stands about 18 or 19 feet above the level of the lake, so you can imagine what a South-East gale can accomplish.[5]

Underground workers must have feared the water's tremendous power, no matter how far-fetched the possibility of blasting through the lakebottom above them. In any case, so many miners left before freezeup "for reasons too numerous to mention" that Frue suspended sinking on the mainland and on Burnt Island. Here two shafts had been blasted out to a depth of about 70 feet in a vain search for silver in paying quantities. The winter of 1872-73 saw all miners at work on Silver Islet, including those with families on the mainland.

Early next spring Frue launched an international campaign to attract a permanent underground workforce. As part of the plan, Thomas Macfarlane visited Norway on a hiring mission. He carried with him one-year contracts, which miners Christian Anderson Konerud and Ole H. Thorsdalen signed.

In preparation for the expected influx of Norwegians and Cornishmen, Frue posted a notice dated May 1, 1873 outlining rules of employment. A jobseeker found he'd work a 60-hour week, that the office would assign him a number for payroll purposes and that the shift schedule for the following week could be viewed only on Saturday, between the hours of 4 and 5 o'clock. He also noted that winter employment had to be arranged by October 15, long before close of navigation.

On being hired, he'd receive a Boarding Ticket for one of the boardinghouses. Mealtimes were scheduled to fit working hours of 7 a.m. to noon and 1 p.m. to six, with breakfast at 6:10, dinner at 12:10, and supper at 6:15. For workmen living on the mainland, the tug left the dock at 6:45 a.m. for day shift and 5:40 p.m. for night shift. The only place on the Islet for relaxation was the reading room, in a building that housed the hospital on its second floor.

To some of the men Rule 7 sounded like a challenge:

All employees at work on Silver Islet will be required to pass through the Watchman's tower, in going to or leaving said Islet. When leaving, they will be subject to search, and will be required to remove boots, coat, hat, etc.

Fines were set at $10 for refusing to submit to search, $5 for drunkenness and $5 for disorderly conduct in a boardinghouse.

May 1873: Depth Of Shaft About 235 Feet

The Norwegian contracts, like so many immigration schemes, proved a disaster. Frue denied the newcomers' requests to break the contracts and return home,

I _Ole H. Thorsdale_ at present residing at _Kongsberg,_ hereby declare that I am a skilled and able-bodied _Miner_ and hereby bind and oblige myself to work as such diligently and faithfully and without being guilty of drunkeness or other misbehavior in the employment of the **The Silver Islet Mining Company**, at the Silver Islet Mine, Lake Superior, Province of Ontario and Dominion of Canada for the space of _One_ year, from and after the first day of June next, working ten hours of each day, Sundays excluded, and do also hereby bind and oblige myself to repay said Company the moneys which they may have advanced towards paying the travelling expences of myself and effects from Christiania to Silver Islet, provided always that said Company fullfills the following Conditions which are part and portion of this Contract:

1. That the Company advance the amount of Money Necessary to pay the Passage of myself and effects from Christiania to Silver Islet.

2. That said Company or its Cashier pays over to me at the end of each Calendar Month the sum of _Fifty_ Dollars Gold or its equivalent after deducting from it fourteen Dollars for Board and lodging, if such are provided by the Company; half a Dollar for medical attendance, and a sum not exceeding Twelve Dollars in part repayment of the Company's outlay for passage money for myself and my effects.

Kongsberg den 16de April 1873.

Huge K. Rua   **Witness:**   _Ole H. Thorsdalen_

Henrik M Vad.   **Witness:**

even though he complained bitterly about their ineptitude as miners. "The men by taking knapsacks with them in the morning would be able to take up on their backs at night all the ground they had broken during the day", he wrote.

Difficulties in communication caused problems too. Some of the other miners "refused to work in the company of men who would fire off their blasts without giving the regular warning to others". These employees gave ten days' notice, as required, and Frue noted sadly, "I saw many of my old tried miners going."

As for "our last assortment of Cornishmen", after only one day on the job they either left or went on strike:

> As to the reasons offered, they were as many and as opposed to compromise as Quills on a Porcupine. The longest and strongest quills appeared to be the poor board, foul air in the mine and the payment of passage money to this place.

> There is a wonderful difference in the sensitive organizations of Cornish miners. Among this lot there were three well marked classes each of which could put up with two of the above evils but was totally incapable of bearing up under the third.[6]

Frue offered to pay the fare of those who stayed and almost half of the men took up his offer. The rest refused to work underground at Silver Islet under any conditions.

By the end of July Frue had sent William Savard to other mining centres to recruit workers at a commission of $5 a head. Correspondence between the two men indicates that the mine was severely shorthanded. Frue asked for 15-20 axemen and the same number of labourers, as well as 30-40 miners. He expressly requested that miners be of mixed nationalities. The chief inducement to workers was a free pass from Collingwood aboard a passenger steamer, second class accommodation.[7]

November 1873: Depth Of Shaft 292 Feet

On October 24 a major setback took place at 292 feet. The drills hit an underground spring and water poured into the shaft at the rate of 80 gallons a minute. Work on the shaft ceased. Frue ordered the engine run at extra speed in order to power the current pumps – 5-inch and 6-inch draw lifts – and to raise barrels of water on the skip. These procedures held the water in check most of the time so that work could continue in a winze* 40 feet below the fourth level at a depth of 252 feet. Even though the miners were interrupted several times "by the water gaining on the pumps", they succeeded in sinking the winze another ten feet.

Meanwhile Frue telegraphed a Detroit firm to build a 12-inch plunger pump. The firm shipped it November 14 on the *City of Fremont*. Alas, the ship froze in at Houghton and the 8-inch plunger pump on hand had to suffice for the winter as a supplement to those pumps already in place.

Putting the pump in working order took till January 8, 1874 "owing to frequent breakings of the rods and connecting chains, caused by the extra speed at which the pump was worked". Mining resumed a few days later and there was no further trouble with flooding.

A massive double engine had been installed over the summer, its cylinders measuring 20 x 48 inches, as well as three new boilers. The work required a deep foundation in the lake, a task Frue described as "slow, tedious and expensive". On July 30 he reported the masonry work well under way:

* A winze is a shaft not directly connected with the surface.

The bedplates, cylinders and pillar blocks of the new engine were put in place, but they have again to be disturbed as more chipping and fitting is necessary to accommodate the pistons and their connections to the crank movements.[8]

The cribs had also been extended eastward, behind the breakwater, to form the foundations for three new boardinghouses – the residential section of the Islet.

The fall sou'easters played havoc with the Islet's installations again in 1873. One storm caused $2,000 damage in mid-November. Another, more fierce, set the company back an estimated $9,000. It tore away about 350 feet of submerged cribs and 60 feet of the main breakwater – 20,000 feet of timber, 7½ tons of bolts and 5,000 tons of rock – and demolished the blacksmith shop which stood behind the breakwater. "Rocks were whirled around the islet like hailstones",[9] Frue noted ruefully as he surveyed the damage to the exteriors of buildings.

Notice to Workmen at Silver Islet, May 1, 1873.

NOTICE

All persons seeking employment here, are requested to read the following rules before making application for work, as they will be strictly enforced:

1. Persons employed at this mine must immediately report to the office, and obtain a number.

2. Employees are required to call at the office on Saturday evening of each week, between the hours of 4:00 and 5:00 o'clock, for the purpose of ascertaining the time required for them, for the week ending on Friday. Should they fail to do so, the time as returned, will be deemed correct.

3. Boarding-house keepers permitting an employee to board in their house, who has not obtained a "Boarding Ticket" will not be allowed to collect the same through the office.

4. Any employee changing his "Boarding House" during the month must first give notice to his "Boarding Boss," and obtain from the office another Ticket, or the board bills as returned, will be charged against him.

5. Ten days after the issue of "Due-bills" will be allowed the parties receiving them, to examine and report errors.

6. A strict observance of the following rules will be required, otherwise no corrections in accounts will be made.

7. All employees at work on Silver Islet, will be required to pass through the watchman's tower, in going to or leaving said islet. When leaving, they will be subject to search and will be required to remove boots, coat, hat, etc., to facilitate the labors of the Watchman in the performance of his duty. A fine of $10.00 will be imposed for any violation of this rule.

8. Any person detected in stealing silver from the Islet, will be prosecuted to the extent of the law.

9. Any employee found intoxicated on these premises, will be fined $5.00, and be liable to dismissal, at the option of the foreman in charge. A like fine will be imposed for disorderly conduct in any if the Boarding Houses.

10. Boarding Houses will serve meals at the following hours: Breakfast, at 6:10 o'clock, A.M., Dinner, at 12:10 o'clock, P.M. , and Supper, at 6:15 o'clock, P.M.

11. All employees will be required to be upon the ground where they are to work, to commence promptly at 7:00 o'clock A.M., and at 1:00 o'clock, P.M., – ten hours being a day.

12. All employers at work on scows, will be under charge of the Watchman, when on the Islet.

13. Ten days notice will be required of any one wanting a settlement, from the opening of navigation to October 15th.

14. Any employee wishing to leave before the close of navigation must give notice of his intention, on or before October 15th, which notice will entitled him to a settlement on the – day of November.

15. All employees whose services are not required during the winter, will be notified on the 15th of October and their settlement given them on the – of November.

16. All employees engaged after November – will be guaranteed steady employment, weather permitting, until June 1st, 18–, providing they conduct themselves properly, and render faithful service.

17. Employees continuing at work after November –, (who have not been notified that their services are not wanted,) shall be considered as evidence that they bind themselves to work until June 1st, 18–.

18. Any employee losing his number, must report the same to the office at once.

19. The tug will leave the dock every morning at 6 o'clock, and 45 minutes; and every evening, at 5 o'clock, and 40 minutes for the purpose of conveying workmen to and from Silver Islet.

W.M. B. FRUE

Silver Islet,
Ont., May 1st, 1873

CHAPTER 13

INDUSTRY IN TRANSITION

evelopment of the Silver Islet Mine played an important part in mechanizing the North American mining industry. Use of the Burleigh compressed air drill in 1872, for example, led to development of improved models specifically designed for mining, like the Rand and the Ingersoll.[1]

In addition, a new invention was developed and tested at Silver Islet. The necessity for treating stamp rock on site inspired Frue to experiment with a concentrating machine, which he ultimately patented as the Frue Vanner.

The value of packing ore* ranged anywhere from $400 to $7,000, averaging about $1,500 a ton. Costs included smelting at $100 a ton, plus freight and insurance. A trial shipment of stamp rock, on the other hand, assayed at between $45 and $50 a ton.[2] Sending raw stamp rock to Wyandotte was out of the question.

At the end of 1872, upwards of 11,000 tons of stamp rock lay on Silver Islet awaiting refining: a potential $495,000. Frue felt the return from this rock alone would more than offset the cost of a stamp mill on site. Sibley agreed, and during the summer of 1873 the two men "caused experiments to be made in Colorado, Nevada, Wyandotte, New York, and at the mine" to see which equipment might be the most efficient for treating Silver Islet's stamp rock.

They chose a typical Lake Superior concentrating mill – two Blake crushers to break the rock into egg-sized chunks and ten Fraser & Chalmers batteries of five stamps each to hammer the chunks into fine particles. These particles mixed with water were called "slimes". Frue Vanners were designed to separate the silver particles from the rest of the slimes by a mechanical process.

A key part for his experimental model arrived from Montreal in November 1873: a 27-foot belt of wide India rubber. Frue mounted the belt on rollers set in a wooden frame so that 12 feet of it formed a "table". The belt moved two ways. Every minute it rolled ahead 100 inches and shook side-to-side 200 times. A spray of water washed the lighter particles away, at the same time allowing the heavy silver to remain on the belt until the end of the cycle, when it dropped into a container as "shining sand".[3]

---

* Ore considered rich enough to ship to the smelter, that is valued at more than the total shipping and handling cost, was called packing ore. Anything less, but still worth processing on site, was dubbed stamp rock.

SILVER ISLET 79

The lower set of Frue Vanners in Silver Islet Mining Company's stamp mill on the mainland.

In order to test the vanner, Frue dammed Sibley Creek to provide water power to run the belt. Then he had a small building constructed creekside to house his invention. Here, close to home, he conducted a series of tests assayed by a Mr. McDonald of Prince Arthur's Landing. By March he was ready for a public demonstration and invited Judge Van Norman, among others, to attend "an experiment with my concentrating machine."

The trial proved eminently successful, with 90 percent of the silver separating from the slimes. No similar equipment could claim such a high rate of recovery. Frue continued making modifications and finally, on October 26, 1874, he filed Canada Patent #3974.[4] Twenty-two Frue Vanners were eventually built and installed in the stamp mill, which began operating at half-capacity the following spring.

The stamp mill, which cost $93,742 to build, operated only 2½ years of its 8-year life span. This view is from the west.

The mill had taken a year and $93,742 to complete under the supervision of mechanical engineer W. T. Forster, assisted by his brother, Theodore. Besides the crushers, stamps and vanners, the huge frame structure housed a 250 horse-power engine powered by four steam boilers. Its capacity was about 60 tons a day. Prominent exterior features were a smokestack, a reserve of ore in untidy heaps and three jackladders or friction hoists to lift the ore to the top story.

A wire cable to move the ore cars extended along a railway track from the top story down to the scow landing a thousand feet away, west of the dock. Each scow could carry ten ore cars, and was towed back and forth to the Islet by one of the tugs.

At the Islet, workmen in the rockhouse sorted the packing ore from the stamp rock, tossing the latter into a waiting ore car. Once loaded, the car was pulled by a yoke of oxen along an inclined railway track to the slip to await loading.

The mill provided work for teenaged boys at $8 to $10 a month. Men did the heavy work, like breaking the ore with sledges into pieces weighing a pound or less. It took two boys to feed the crushers and six men to feed the stamps. Below,

Workmen on Silver Islet loaded stamp rock into ore cars for transporting to the mill. Boys were hired to help with the lighter work.

three men on the upper floor and four boys on the lower floor tended the Frue Vanners, which were arranged in two sets, one below the other. Waste slimes flowed into Lake Superior.[5]

From the time the shrill broken note of the mill's steam whistle announced startup in May 1875, until the fires were allowed to go out in November 1876, the mill ran 24,446 tons through its machines at a cost of $48,145 or $1.97 a ton. The original estimate had been $1.50 a ton. The concentrates thus produced yielded silver worth $225,180 or $9.21 a ton.[6] The assay of $45 to $50 a ton for the trial shipment of stamp rock was far richer than subsequent deliveries. Evidently the projections were too optimistic.

Shortly after startup of the mill Frue resigned, effective August 1, 1875. The move came abruptly. His letter of resignation stated only that "circumstances over which I have no control, dictate and compel the adoption of the present course." His reason may well have been to promote the Frue Vanner.

He appointed as his agent John Adams, first graduate of the Columbia School of Mines. Soon descriptions of the invention began appearing in key journals. Fraser & Chalmers of Chicago purchased the patent and introduced Frue Vanners throughout North America, including the Alaska goldfields. An English manufacturer, J. T. Jordon Sons & Commons, distributed them internationally as part of a Continuous Ore-Dressing Plant.[7]

Frue not only participated in perfecting new mechanisms for treating ores, he also pioneered in applying existing technology to mining. Under his supervision the Silver Islet Mine grossed $1,936,004 in silver;[8] most of the difficult marine construction took place; and the mainland assumed its present character.

Table 5.
Product of Stamp Mill,
May 1875 to November 1876

PRODUCT OF STAMP MILL, MAY 1875 – NOV. 1876

Month.		Tons rock stamped.	Product in concentrates. Tons. Lbs.	Total ounces of silver contained in same.	Total cost of dressing.
May	1875	541	11.1454	10,210	$1,237.69
June	1875	1,065	25.212	17,552	2,019.89
July	1875	1,079	28.104	19,125	2,427.33
August	1875	762	20.1100	11,238	2,302.78
September	1875	1,505	35.182	17,804	2,990.85
October	1875	1,678	37.843	14,415	2,840.15
December	1875	1,642	31.817	11,548	3,172.26
January	1876	1,556	30.1821	15,990	3,089.96
February	1876	1,421	28.1312	16,346	2,944.89
March	1876	1,690	32.651	15,754	3,288.60
April	1876	645	10.1475	4,806	1,788.83
May	1876	1,673	33.583	9,614	3,086.62
June	1876	1,565	33.1288	10,504	2,891.36
July	1876	1,525	41.978	11,757	2,768.47
August	1876	1,600	39.1591	9,527	2,863.04
September	1876	1,505	33.1232	10,060	2,807.17
October	1876	1,500	38.1835	9,234	2,596.26
November	1876	1,494	29.194	11,389	3,093.93
		24,446	541 $\frac{1705}{2000}$	226,873	$18,145.08

Office of WM. B. FRUE,

Silver Islet, Ontario, September 1 1875

Genl. C. L. Stevenson
    Enterprise Mine.
        Black Bay.

Dear Sir.

    I have just returned from Detroit, and the Major has handed me your letter of the 19 ultimo. and I am very much pleased to notice your favorable opinion— Your report to myself has been misplaced therefore I have not had the pleasure of reading it.

    I write now for the purpose of informing. you, that arrangements have been made for the shipment of all ore that will pay transportation to Swansea. Wales—, and leave a small profit; the ore shipped to Wyandotte would be worth about $60⁰⁰ per ton. I mention this so that you may know something of the value of the ore. The Cost of Transportation to Sarnia is as follows. viz.
    Per ton to Montreal $6⁰⁰
              . Swansea   40 Shillings
now what I want is to have every available pound of ore taken at to the Landing

CHAPTER 14

THE END OF AN ERA

rue's tenure from 1870 to 1875 embraced the glory years of Silver Islet, when the community boasted the most successful mining operation as well as the best harbour in the area. The former record stood for many years, but the latter would alter as government plans for the development of transport in Northwestern Ontario changed.

The earliest harbour statistics to separate the east end of Lake Superior from the west end cover the fiscal year ending June 30, 1875. The previous summer John Livingstone began reporting to the new collector at Prince Arthur's Landing, Peter Nicholson, rather than to Sault Ste. Marie. The figures show that the Silver Islet sub-collector accounted for almost 70 percent of customs revenues totalling $10,202, with about 30 percent from Prince Arthur's Landing and a negligible amount from Fort William.[1]

The federal government built its first lighthouse on Lake Superior in 1867, facing out from Nipigon Bay. The structure measured 15 x 18 feet, with a white tower housing three kerosene lamps. Because this navigational aid stood only two miles from St. Ignace island, on Talbot Island, it became known as St. Ignace light.

The first lightkeeper, a Mr. Perry, "perished in the attempt to reach Fort William" after close of navigation in 1868. The story goes that he was so preoccupied with gathering agates that he didn't hear the *Algoma* whistle for him on her last run of the season.[2] Perry's body was found in the bay that bears his name, inside Catholic Point, along with his battered boat. The agates lay scattered underwater.

The following season substantial additions were made to St. Ignace light, doubling the size of its living quarters. The idea was that lightkeeper Thomas Lamphier and his wife could winter on the site rather than risk a boat trip after close of navigation. Lamphier was a veteran on the lake, having captained the Hudson's Bay Company schooner *Whitefish* out of Fort William during the 1840s and 1850s. Unfortunately he died soon after freezeup the first year he tended the light. Mrs. Lamphier had to maintain a lonely vigil over her husband's body until being rescued in the spring.

Andrew Hynes was the keeper in 1872. At close of navigation he extinguished the light and set out for Thunder Bay in an open boat. After 18 days of stormy weather the cold and exhausted man finally ended up at Silver Islet under Dr. Tompkins' care. But it was too late. He died soon afterward from the effects of exposure.

The government decided to abandon St. Ignace light. The death of three keepers had earned it another name, the lighthouse of doom.[3] The next record of a government lighthouse in the region was 1876 at the mouth of the Kaministiquia River. Construction of lighthouses befitting a busy shipping lane, including those at Thunder Cape and Point Porphyry, began almost a decade after the ill-fated Perry first took over St. Ignace light.

The federal decision to construct a transcontinental railway had ushered in a flurry of activity during the early 1870s, and surveys were under way throughout the region. Local responses included construction of the Oliver, Davidson & Co. sawmill on an island opposite Fort William, near the mouth of the Kaministiquia River. The owners had assurances of a contract to cut the railway right-of-way to Savanne, 50 miles westward.

A partner in the mill, P. J. Brown of Ingersoll, became the first reeve of the Municipality of Shuniah at its establishment in 1873. One of his first tasks was to sign a petition in 1874 to the federal government on behalf of Thunder Bay as "the most advantageous point for the terminus of the Canadian Pacific Railway on Lake Superior".[4]

The new Liberal government under Alexander Mackenzie favoured Nipigon Bay as the terminus. Earlier, engineers had recommended this route westward as first choice because it offered two advantages over their second choice, Thunder Bay: flatter terrain and a supportive water route for transportation of workmen and supplies. Both were important economic factors, especially to a government committed to a policy of economy on railway matters.

Nevertheless an alternate site was selected for the terminus, four miles upstream on the Kaministiquia River, surveyed in 1859 as the Town Plot. Here, on June 1, 1875, another partner in the mill, Adam Oliver, turned the first sod for the railway. Contracts had already been awarded to Oliver, Davidson & Co. for the telegraph line, and to Sifton & Ward for railway construction, westward from the Town Plot.

All these events centering around construction of the transcontinental railway signalled the end of an era for Silver Islet. As a company town, its population was limited to the number of employees the mine could support. The harbour had developed rapidly, but only in response to the company's needs. Any future growth depended upon the discovery of another bonanza.

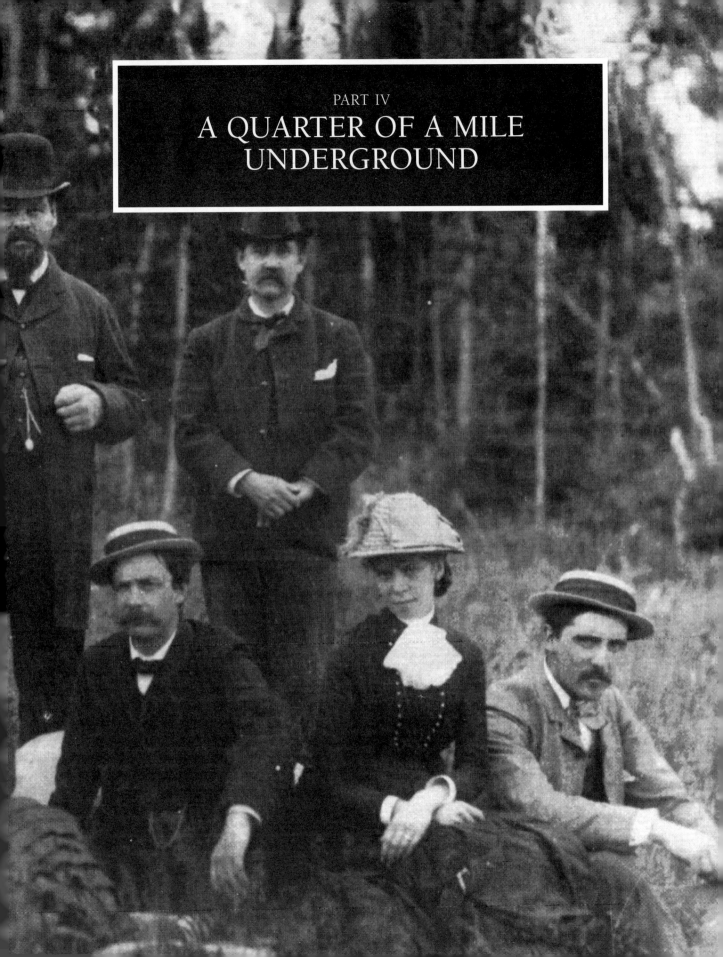

PART IV

A QUARTER OF A MILE
UNDERGROUND

Richard Trethewey (1835–1888)
directed the affairs of Silver Islet Mine as superintendent
from 1875 until its closure in 1884.

RICHARD TRETHEWEY (1835-1888)

The surname Trethewey derives from the family's traditional place of residence in Cornwall, England. The literal translation is "Land of David", with "Tre" coming from Terra (Latin for land) and "thewey" from the Cornish word for David. The name is pronounced with emphasis on the second syllable.

Richard Trethewey had deep roots in Cornwall. He was also the namesake of his father, grandfather and great grandfather. Nevertheless by the early 1860s he had married and emigrated to the United States to work as a mining captain.

Details are sketchy about his early life and training in Cornwall, and also about his activities in the United States. One contemporary described him as a musician and composer. Others noted that he was involved with importing Cornish miners to North America. These immigrants and others like them formed the backbone of the copper mining industry in upper Michigan.

Richard Trethewey went to Silver Islet as mining captain in late 1871 in order to establish the mine as an underground operation. He brought with him his wife Mary Hannah and their five children, all born before the family arrived in Canada.

When he succeeded Frue as superintendent four years later his younger brother, John Trethewey, took over as mining captain. The arrangement must have caused considerable confusion. The brothers looked alike and dressed in similar attire. Their full black beards and derby hats are clearly visible in vintage photographs, hovering in the background more often than not. A closer look reveals that they both wore three-piece suits and carried pocket watches, with fob and chain draped across portly abdomens.

Captain Dick and Captain John, as they were called, remained at Silver Islet as superintendent and mining captain until the mine closed in 1884. Since one or the other had charge of the underground workings during the mine's entire productive lifespan they had intimate knowledge of its development. Unfortunately, only a few of their papers are known to have survived.

Richard Trethewey left Silver Islet in August 1884, and returned for the winter of 1885-86 to close the operation. In between he moved to new silver finds southwest of Port Arthur. As part owner of one of them - Silver Mountain East End - he journeyed to England during the summer of 1886 in an effort to find backing for its development.

Evidently the venture, or perhaps his health, failed. The family moved to Sarnia the same year. He died there on April 7, 1888, at the age of fifty-two.

CHAPTER 15

A SEARCH FOR NEW DIRECTIONS

Silver Islet was the most successful mining operation in the region. Nevertheless when Richard Trethewey became superintendent in 1875 he took over a mine that had experienced disappointing production levels for two years. The shaft plumbed the depths almost 480 feet to the eighth level, but no ore had been found below the seventh level. The company decided to bring in a diamond-tipped exploration drill before sinking further.

In 1872 Frue had advised a disgruntled investor that "we are short-sighted mortals and can't see through the solid rock". Now, just three years later, his successor was doing the next-best thing – bringing up cores of rock from as deep as 293 feet.

The portable drill supplied by the Severance & Holt Company (or later, the American Drill Company, New York) came equipped with a steam boiler but it ran by compressed air underground. The ungainly assortment of sprockets, pulleys and metal pipe represented brand new mining technology, a North American improvement on similar drills developed in Europe for boring railway tunnels.[1]

The apparatus began working November 29, 1875 from an underground position 120 feet south of the shaft, on the eighth level. By the following September a total of 25 holes had been drilled, 21 from the eighth level and four from the ninth level, 560 feet underground.[2] To Trethewey's dismay none of them offered any clues as to the location of the hoped-for bonanza.

On October 1, 1876 the company's books showed a deficit of $335,615 and it became apparent that something had to be done. Head office decided to launch action on two fronts: reassessment of the mine and reorganization of the company.

The three man inspection team for the mine was composed of the treasurer, John J. Marvin of New York, former treasurer Edward Learned, and Carl Oscar Wederkinch, a mining engineer from the Sutro Tunnel Company in Nevada. At this point the future of the mine virtually lay in Wederkinch's hands.[3]

In his opinion the fluctuations in the vein's width, from a foot to 20 feet or more, could be readily explained by the vertical displacement of 80 feet in which the vein material was found.

This diamond drill was used on Silver Islet and other holdings from 1875 to 1880 both underground and above ground.

Wherever the break originally has not been straight, hollow places may have met opposite, making the vein very wide, and where rounded surfaces came together near enough to touch there would be little or no vein for some distance.[4]

Coming upon another large pocket of rich ore was therefore a distinct possibility.

As for the length of the vein along the fault line, he came to the conclusion that the best hope of finding silver was from Silver Islet itself. At the same time he didn't discount that the vein extension crossing Burnt Island and the mainland "might be underlaid with chimneys or deposits of richer ore." Although the diamond drill was used throughout the fall of 1876 and into 1877 to work the vein on Burnt Island and beyond the stamp mill, no rich deposits were discovered.

On Silver Islet the main shaft had been sunk to the ninth level on a vertical plane. However the core samples showed that the vein itself angled eastward about 21 inches every six feet, so that the main shaft had already passed out of it. According to Wederkinch:

> The smaller bodies of silver ore met with in these workings were what might be called drippings from the larger mass found above.[5]

He recommended that an inclined winze be sunk from the ninth level, running very near the centre of the main vein and cutting it at the same angle.

At head office in New York, responsibility for reorganizing the company fell to three directors, William C. Langley and original stockholders George S. Coe and Peleg Hall. On April 3, 1877 they formally organized a new company, the Silver Islet Consolidated Mining and Lands Company, under the laws of New York state. This company absorbed the lands and property of both the Silver Mining Company of Silver Islet and the Ontario Mineral Lands Company.[6] The move did little more than buy time for the mine. And trouble.

Since the latter company owned 55 percent of the stock in the Wyandotte Smelting and Refining Works, the $20,000 debt of the former company was paid in shares. A disagreement about their value resulted in a lawsuit. While the matter was before the courts, head office instructed that ore be sent to Crooke Brothers & Co. of New York,[7] a much smaller facility.

One of Trethewey's first tasks as superintendent had been to reduce the summer work force of 250 men to a winter complement of 100. The following summer of 1876 saw limited activity. The stamp mill, as noted, shut down in the fall. The diamond drill moved underground again, but to the upper part of the mine. The first of six holes was drilled from the fourth level, beginning November 20. Nothing. At the end of March 1877, drilling began on the first level. Then in April an ore bucket fell on miner George McKenzie, killing him instantly.

Meanwhile miners sinking the inclined winze from the ninth level, as advocated by Wederkinch, found a promising lode at the tenth level. It was with mixed emotions that Trethewey had the pumps disconnected below the third level as a temporary economy measure. He laid off most of the men. Company houses stood empty. It seemed as though the mine would close unless a daring engineering experiment was carried out.

The procedure suggested was nothing less than to construct an artificial roof inside the mine in order to keep out the waters of Lake Superior. In this way it was felt that the rich ores near the surface, an estimated half a million dollars worth, could be mined from above without flooding the mine. Plans called for six layers of brick to form arches over both veins and along their junction, at a distance of 60 feet below the lake's surface.[8] After four years of frustration and disappointment it seemed the directors were willing to try anything.

CHAPTER 16

BONANZA AT LAST

T he silver arch, as it was called, never got off the drawing board, although the bricks were ordered and delivered and benches three feet wide were cut in the vein walls as supports. In August 1877 limited mining began again on the first level. Here near the junction of the two veins – the main or west vein and Macfarlane's east vein – the diamond drill brought up a core of rich ore. The find, although small, signalled a turn for the better. By the end of the year, packing ore yielding 23,850 ounces of silver had been extracted.

The second and third levels offered similar results, so that Trethewey ordered the mine pumped out during the summer of 1878. Then in August 1878, a year after the first signs of a turnaround, came the second bonanza. Soon almost 200 men were at work. Empty company houses filled with families once again. W. T. Forster returned from the south shore to supervise the stamp mill, which ran from May through November. The year 1878 ended with a production of almost 600,000 ounces of silver.

Most of the silver mined so far came from within 360 feet of the surface, that is above the sixth level. The first bonanza, worked out under Frue, extended 335 feet downward in the shape of an irregular pear, and yielded two million ounces of silver. The second bonanza in 1878 resembled an inverted cone. It hung from the third level, near the junction of the two veins, like a giant plumb bob, with its widest point 50 feet across and petering out at the fifth level, or 285 feet.

Office

THE SILVER ISLET CONSOLIDATED MINING AND LANDS COMPANY,

52 BROADWAY,

TRUSTEES.

Edward Learned, Pittsfield, Mass.
William A. Booth, New York.
William C. Langley,   "
Geo. S. Coe,   "
Peleg Hall,   "
C. A. Trowbridge,   "
R. E. Strong,   "
Jno. J. Marvin,   "
Geo. Snell, Boston, Mass.
A. H. Sibley, Detroit, Mich.

New-York, June 17   1878

A winze in the middle of the deposit to the 4th level, sixty feet, was sunk literally through native silver, the metal standing out boldly from the four walls of the winze.

In the breast of the drift it stood out in great arborescent masses in the shape of hooks and spikes, in gnarled, drawn out and twisted bunches.[1]

Miners wore a hard hat of sorts. Their only illumination underground was a candle pasted with clay to the front of their hats.

Since the winze plumbed the lode itself, some of the ore had to be left underground in the form of support pillars, both vertical and horizontal. Still, the deposit yielded 800,000 ounces of silver in all.

Silver Islet ore included the metallic minerals native silver, silver glance (also called argentite), galena (today's sphalerite), copper and iron pyrites with marcasite. Whenever silver occurred, carbon in the form of graphite was always associated with it. Native silver glistened with a silvery sheen, tarnishing black in air or water. The orebodies themselves were encased in vein material of "calcite, quartz and dolomite, the latter varying in colour from cream to pink, according to the varying amounts of manganese."[2]

Ore from the first bonanza also included macfarlanite, isolated by Thomas Macfarlane as "reddish-coloured grains". He assayed the substance before 1870 and found it to contain about 78 percent silver.[3] Sibley named the supposed new metal macfarlanite in his honour.

The second bonanza contained two similar compounds isolated by Professor Henry Wurtz of New York. He named one of them huntilite after T. Sterry Hunt of Montreal, and the other animikite for the animikie rocks in which it was found.

The three terms macfarlanite, huntilite and animikite were widely accepted throughout the mining community, and in 1881 assayer F. E. Lowe described them as "the principle producing silver ores of the mine."[4] Today they are discredited as individual minerals. Animikite is described as a mixture of silver and dyscrasite, huntilite as arsenian silver, and macfarlanite as containing silver, galena and niccolite.

Trethewey was tremendously encouraged by discovery of the second bonanza. To his brother, John, had fallen his former position of underground captain. The two men were dubbed Captain Dick and Captain John to tell them apart. Together they became convinced of Wederkinch's theory that the best chance of finding a third bonanza lay in the main vein, along the fault line. They determined to carry out his recommendation to continue sinking the inclined winze below the ninth level.

Both men understood the implications for miners as the workings deepened. The accepted means of ascent and descent was a ladder and the only source of air were pipes running from the surface. Most underground activity having resulted from brute force, good air was essential

Miners wore a hard hat of sorts, with a brim to catch any wax that might drip from the candle attached to its front. Found in the mine was a "sticky, brownish-grey clayey material"[5] admirably suited for pasting the candle to the hat and to the rock face of the workplace. This flickering flame provided the

Table 5.
Minerals Reported from
Silver Islet

MINERALS REPORTED FROM SILVER ISLET

Mineral	Formula	References
"Animikite"	mixture	2, 4
Annabergite	$Ni_3(AsO_4)_2 \cdot 8H_2O$	2, 3
Argentite	Ag_2S	1, 2, 3
"Arquerite"	mercurian silver	4
Barite	$BaSO_4$	3
Breithauptite	NiSb	4
Calcite	$CaCO_3$	1, 2, 3
Chalcopyrite	$CuFeS_2$	1, 2, 3
Chlorargyrite	AgCl	1, 2, 3
Chlorite group		6
Cobaltite	CoAsS	3
Dolomite	$CaMg(CO_3)_2$	3
Domeykite	Cu_3As	2, 3
Erythrite	$Co_3(AsO_4)2 \cdot 8H_2O$	2, 3
Fluorite	CaF_2	6
Galena	PbS	1, 2, 3
Graphite	C	1, 2, 6
Gypsum	$CaSO_4 \cdot 2H_2O$	5
"Huntilite"	mixture	2, 4
"Macfarlanite"	mixture	2, 4
Marcasite	FeS_2	3
Nickeline	NiAs	1, 2, 3
Pyrargyrite	Ag_3SbS_3	1
Pyrite	FeS_2	1, 2
Pyrolusite	MnO_2	3
Quartz	SiO_2	1, 2, 3
Rhodochrosite	$MnCO_3$	1, 3
Silver	Ag	1, 2, 3
Skutterudite	$CoAS_{2-3}$	1, 3
Sphalerite	(Zn,Fe)S	1, 2, 3
Stephanite	Ag_5SbS_4	1
Tetrahedrite	$(Cu,Fe)_{12}Sb_4S_{13}$	2, 3
Wurtzite	(Zn,Fe)S	7

References: (1) McDermott, 1909; (2) Macfarlane, 1879; (3) Tanton, 1931; (4) Parsons and Thomson, 1921; (5) Satterly, 1977; (6) Ingall, 1889; (7) Lance Hampel, personal communication.

only illumination underground.

Safety features such as steel-toed footwear did not exist. A miner donned ordinary boots, pants and shirt before starting a shift and afterward he hung them to dry in the changehouse. A sympathetic visitor in October 1875 noted that miners now worked eight-hour shifts rather than ten:

> The miner's regalia dirty and damp, if not wet, is not inviting, and none should begrudge $2.25 per day; there is many a brave, cheerful heart under the miner's unprepossessing uniform.[6]

Only two months later, on December 28, some of these brave cheerful hearts underwent a trial by fire. A crew working on the eighth level drilled into a water hole. One of the men plucked a candle from the wall for a closer look, unaware that the crevice also contained flammable gas under pressure. Suddenly, with a muffled roar, a giant flame shot 40 feet down the drift. Miners dropped to the ground, uninjured but terribly frightened.

When the flame subsided, they tried again. This time the gas ignited within 40 feet of the hole. A sheet of flame filled the drift to within three feet of the floor, and also jetted 150 feet toward the shaft, the source of air. As soon as the fire died down a little, someone crept along the floor and plugged the hole with a wooden peg. The next day enough gas still escaped around the peg to throw a continuous flame a foot long.[7]

Pockets of water and gas were found together throughout the mine's workings, a phenomenon unusual in the mining world. Below the eighth level the water was so caustic blisters formed on skin on contact with it. Analysis by F. E. Lowe showed high concentrations of calcium chloride, nearly a pint of "very acrid and deliquescent salt" to every two gallons of liquid.[8] The gas was never analyzed, though it turned up elsewhere throughout the region. The suggestion is that it was methane.

In the upper reaches of Silver Islet mine, down to the ninth level at 560 feet, the distance between levels varied considerably. The inclined winze plunged downward from the ninth level with each subsequent level representing 100 feet, that is the tenth level measured 660 feet underground, the eleventh 760 feet, and so on. During 1879 miners succeeded in sinking the inclined winze to 843 feet, and in 1880 to 974 feet, beyond the thirteenth level.

At the thirteenth level, 90 feet along the south drift, the men cut into a pocket of "very rich silver". Trethewey felt certain his faith had been justified. This find resembled the second bonanza in every respect. It occurred where the diorite dike made contact with surrounding slates and it showed native silver at the top and huntilite and macfarlanite immediately below. He ordered the inclined winze continued to the surface as the "new" main shaft in order to facilitate pumping and hoisting operations.

CHAPTER 17

LIFE AND DEATH MATTERS

During the summer of 1880 the company store exhibited a rich 91-pound specimen of Silver Islet ore with the claim that it assayed at 12,004 ounces to the ton. Other specimens were officially displayed at the Philadelphia Centennial in 1876 and two years later at the Paris Fair. At Silver Islet itself, a collection at the minesite in 1875 showed the differences between its own ores and those found elsewhere in the region.

At the unofficial level, pieces of ore seemed to be widely distributed among a knowledgeable subculture. A visitor to Prince Arthur's Landing noted this phenomenon and published his description of a typical bar scene in 1876:

> one [person] talks of Silver Islet, another of Shuniah, the Cornish, 3A, the Bruce Mines, Thunder Bay, or Shebandowan, and each pulls from his pocket a specimen of the ore...

> Various as the specimens may be, and, to the unskilled, scarcely differing in structure and appearance, yet our friends here will at once name the mine whence they came.[1]

At Silver Islet Landing, visitors were accommodated at a two-story hotel near the dock run by Robert and Elizabeth Down. A brother, William Down, arrived in 1877. The following year the Downs left Silver Islet to return to England and the family of a deceased mining captain named Everington took over the hotel.

The proprietor of the President's mansion changed too. A. H. Sibley died July 10, 1878 following a stroke. He and Frue happened to be together in New York at the time, making arrangements to back a Montana gold mine. Frue accompanied the body of his friend to Detroit for burial.

Edward Learned replaced Sibley as president, but it appears as though the family of Learned's successor, John J. Marvin, made a more lasting impression:

> His charming and beautiful wife, a magnificent pianiste and graduate of Vienna conservatory,

and Mrs. Marvin's pretty and attractive nieces the Misses Florence and Emma Lane of Kingston, Rhode Island, together with many others of art, military and political distinction were resident guests.[2]

A billiard table had been set up in "Trelawney", the servants' quarters next door. This was a unique building in that there was no indoor stairway between the ground floor and the upstairs. No doubt the billiard table was a favourite haunt of Lieutenants Marvin and Coe of West Point Military Academy.

Bonfires on Burnt Island provided a popular evening entertainment for the young people. Here Silver Islet's élite and their guests enjoyed a cookout of roast potatoes and "planked" fish, that is Lake Superior trout or whitefish served on a wooden board. "The culinary operations," Janey Livingstone recalled, "were performed by our trusted servant, John Messiah, generally known as *Omishomiss*.* Later the group sang around the campfire, accompanied by James C. Hill on the accordion and whoever cared to join in with mouth organs, banjos or kazoos.

The mining company arranged a picnic for employees and their families each summer. Indoor gatherings took place in private homes or in the schoolhouse. Once the teacher, Miss Hayes, directed her pupils in a summer play titled "Cinderella", issuing invitations to Prince Arthur's Landing residents through the newspaper, *Thunder Bay Sentinel*. One winter the craze was skating on Surprise Lake.

Arrangements for winter mail had improved only slightly since Frue's frustrating experiences of the 1871-72 season. Preliminary work on a "mail track" to Pigeon River had begun in 1872, along with surveys of the three townships through which it would pass – Blake, Crooks and Pardee.** Construction of the Pigeon River Road started the following year, along the approximate route of today's Highway 61.

According to the inspector's report the route offered little more than a visible ribbon of cleared ground to follow for a snow road. Stumps were cut too high, culverts were missing and levelling had not been carried out.[3]

Weather determined when and if the mails got through during the entire active period of Silver Islet Mine. Most years the Pigeon River Road served as a route for men on snowshoes and toboggans. During the open winter of 1877-78, however, the carrier rode a horse because of inadequate snowfall. He found "the last five [miles] were never finished, and it is impossible for a horse to get through." Carriers in other years had been able to cover this section over the ice.

In 1875-76 John Livingstone received $940 to arrange weekly mail service from December 1 to May 15. He subcontracted the job, 61 miles each way, to a Silver Islet resident named Joseph Whalen. Whalen and his dog team soon became a familiar sight, with Tray, Blanche, Sweetheart, Thunder and Leader

* John Messiah was an Ojibway, and *Omishomiss* an Ojibway word meaning "grandfather".
** Named for Edward Blake, Adam Crooks and T. B. Pardee, all Ontario cabinet members in 1872.

hitched single file to a canvas-sided birch toboggan two feet wide. Paul Messiah went along as assistant.

The Port Arthur and Silver Islet Royal Mail toboggan and dog team is photographed in Port Arthur in 1883–84.

The entourage left Silver Islet at noon Friday bound for Prince Arthur's Landing, returning Monday or Tuesday. Once, under almost perfect weather conditions, they flew over the 45 miles from Pigeon River to Prince Arthur's Landing in about seven hours. Whalen boasted that this was "the fastest trip on record."[4]

The problem of regular winter mail delivery was not solved with the reported construction of a "Silver Islet Road" during the summer of 1882. Perhaps this road was as rudimentary as the one to Pigeon River. In any case, only after the mine closed did mail service improve to Port Arthur and Fort William. The reason was completion in 1885 of the Canadian Pacific Railway along the north shore.

On the trail, or down the mine, or at home, illness and accident posed constant threats. Dr. Tompkins died of an unspecified illness on January 11, 1879, shortly after guiding the community through an epidemic of scarlet fever. His replacement, Dr. Lorne C. Campbell of Toronto, arrived early in February. Mrs. Tompkins had her husband's body placed in a special metal case and brought to Houghton for burial on the opening of navigation.

Around this time was founded the Silver Islet Employees Benefit Society,[5] a scheme to help with expenses in the case of a member's death or illness. In the days before life insurance and medical plans, workmen's compensation and widows' allowance, such a group offered the breadwinner and his family a certain measure of security.

For dues of 50 cents a month, each member was paid $5 a week while unable to work because of illness or accident. Death benefit amounted to $200. The Society's constitution and by-laws make fascinating reading, especially in terms of the moral judgments included in them.

Claims would not be considered, for example, for "sickness or accident

CONSTITUTION

—AND—

BY-LAWS

—OF THE—

Silver Islet Employees Benefit Society

Established Sept. 1st, 1880.

H. T. Butler, Printer, Times Office, Stratford, Ontario.

1880.

brought on by fighting, except in self-defence, wrestling, intoxication, debauchery and other misconduct." Special rules for employees doing blasting included a list of acceptable tools for uncharging a missed hole. And the final by-law, predictably, carried provisions for "Disposal of Funds in Event of the Works Closing Down."

The Society began by electing 12 officers in September 1880, headed by Thomas H. Trethewey as president. Trethewey called himself a mariner, unlike his distant cousins who were mining captains. He first came to Prince Arthur's Landing in November 1871 from Bruce Mines, with orders to build Thomas Marks' new dock, store and warehouse. He soon established a business repairing tugs and boats and it was in this capacity he worked at Silver Islet in 1878, rebuilding the *Silver Spray* which had been badly damaged in late 1875. In 1880 he was working on the inclined winze.

Trethewey was a widower with four young children, his wife, Levina, having recently died in childbirth. One of the vice-presidents, Martin Sullivan, became a first-time father the month of the election. Of the other officers, night watchman William and Lizzie Clarke had three children; Captain William and Jessie Craig had four; and blacksmith John and Mary Jilbert had

Small children seem out of place in an industrial setting, but Willie and Maggie (seated right) actually lived on Silver Islet while their parents, J.W. and Helen Cross, ran one of the boardinghouses. Their brother Harry was born on Silver Islet, and so was Lulu, daughter of James and Lizzie Bailey.

five. All felt a need for the kind of protection the Society offered.

Their one-year term of office had terrifying moments. A fall storm destroyed the breakwater and sent water down the shaft with each wave that broke over it. Two men volunteered to go down and warn the miners. More than an hour later they began surfacing "all drenched to the skin and so benumbed by the cold and toil that they could scarcely hold on to the rungs of the ladders."

On the mainland, a group of observers climbed to a lookout to see how the storm was affecting the mine.

> We saw to our horror the waves rushing right through the middle of the Islet between the machinery house and shaft of the mine and the boarding-house...

> We saw two buildings go down before the waves, and as the storm permitted we noticed the breach of water widen more and more while dense clouds of spray shot up against and over the houses, shops and steam-engine house, threatening to engulf them...

> The waves poured over the destroyed breakwater carrying logs and stones upon their crests.[6]

Miraculously, nobody was killed.

Shortly afterward a fall injured three men seriously. Richard and John Trethewey were standing on a staging with miners named Dennis Higgins and John Ferguson. Suddenly the staging gave way. Richard Trethewey saved himself by hanging to the side, but the others tumbled a dozen feet to the rocks below.

Then two miners suffered burns in February when they drilled into a crevice of gas under pressure. If all five injured men belonged to the Silver Islet Employees Benefit Society, the funds came under severe strain.

CHAPTER 18

COUNTDOWN TIME

T he bricks ordered for the silver arch, and never used, were still in storage when a fire in Prince Arthur's Landing levelled St. Andrew's Catholic Church there in 1881. Trethewey promptly donated the bricks to Father Baxter to rebuild the church. The first mass in the new church took place in August 1881.

The support given the pioneer priest had been noted by a visiting Jesuit as early as October 1875:

Captain T., who superintends these works, allows Fr. Baxter to come first in the religious services of Silver Islet, though he himself is a Protestant. The reason he gives is that the priest needs no breakfast before his service.[1]

Silver Islet Mine's officers in 1882 included Richard Trethewey, centre rear.

Quotes like these make one wish Trethewey had left correspondence or other clues to his character.

The year 1881 was a busy one at Silver Islet. First of all, there was a major cleanup to carry out after the storm. Then repairs had to be made to the break-water and other structures. During the summer a new feature appeared on the skyline, nothing less than a new shafthouse over the inclined shaft.*

Richard Trethewey supervised the sinking of the inclined shaft and construction of its shaft house, which towered over the previous one. The building with the stone foundation housed the engines.

The imposing edifice towered over its predecessor, abutting the southwest corner at an angle. Clearly, Trethewey held high hopes for large amounts of rich ore passing up the inclined shaft, now the mine's main shaft. In order to distinguish it from the vertical shaft, the latter was belatedly called the Macfarlane Shaft. The diggings had long ago reached the ore Macfarlane sought in 1869.

July 25, 1881 was a red letter day for Silver Islet in that for the second time a Governor General of Canada paid the community a visit. The Marquess of Lorne stopped there on his way to British Columbia. Under terms of union reached a decade earlier, the federal government had promised a railway to the Pacific within ten years. Lorne's task was to convince the province to wait a little longer.

That July morning the *Silver Spray* steamed through heavy seas into the comparative calm of Silver Islet harbour. John Livingstone, as government representative, greeted the vice regal visitor. A rich specimen of ore was presented to him. After a short tour, he boarded the yacht once again.

Lorne seemed more impressed by the failure of the Montreal Mining Company to exploit the find than by what he saw at the mine. He commented only on the scenery, comparing Thunder Bay to his native Scotland:

* The inclined winze could be called a shaft now that it reached the surface.

Whoever has seen the Treshnish group of the Hebrides and the headlands of Mull, can form some idea of the appearance of Thunder Cape and its sister island.[2]

Later, at Prince Arthur's Landing, he likened that village to San Francisco. The Pacific port was not only located on the world's largest landlocked harbour, it was the terminus of North America's first transcontinental railway. Residents can hardly be blamed if they read more into his remarks than he intended. After all, hadn't their community been named for Lorne's brother-in-law, Prince Arthur?

"The chief difference being," he continued, still comparing Prince Arthur's Landing with San Francisco, "that your harbour is reached through a Silver instead of a Golden Gate."[3] The reference to Silver Islet as an example of the area's mining potential captured many imaginations. The catch phrase "Silver Gateway" appeared in promotional literature for many years afterward.

Lorne was able to travel westward by rail for 200 miles, to end-of-track at Wabigoon Lake. Railway construction to Winnipeg was now expected to be completed within a year or so. Even more important for Prince Arthur's Landing was the Macdonald government's insistence that the railway should be an all-Canadian route along the north shore of Lake Superior. If this plan materialized, which it did by 1885, the future of the community would no longer hang in the balance.

As the fortunes of Prince Arthur's Landing waxed, so those of Silver Islet waned. Incorporation of the Canadian Pacific Railway Company in 1881 inspired head office to petition the company to extend the railway as far as Silver Islet. Their pamphlet titled "A Communication Addressed to the Hon. Duncan McIntyre, Vice-President, respecting Silver Islet Harbor as a Lake Superior Terminus of the Canadian Pacific Railroad ..." included a detailed "Plan of the Village of Silver Islet and Silver Islet Mine."[4] The railway was never built and hopes for the future of the mine itself were fading.

The expected third bonanza petered out after yielding $30,000 in silver.[5] Reports of new strikes continued to appear in the press but each find proved disappointing. The stamp mill got up steam for the last time in July 1882 for a four-month run.

The value of silver production for the year 1882 amounted to only $14,143, and the report to shareholders was blunt:

It is useless to disguise the disappointment of the directors that thus far ... the long looked-for bonanza has not been reached.[6]

Liabilities had already soared to more than $100,000.

Then, at nine o'clock the night of January 10, 1883, one of the boilers exploded in the enginehouse. Engineer William Beatty suffered severe scalds and fireman Samuel McFachern died from injuries.

Young Samuel had grown up at Silver Islet and worked for the company off and on since he was a lad. His parents, Duncan and Rachel McEachern, spent the summers in charge of Thunder Cape lighthouse now. They chose Silver Islet cemetery as the final resting place for their eldest son.

Damage to the steam plant took almost three weeks to repair. During this time the pumps weren't fully operative and water in the mine rose 330 feet. On March 15, when the shaft was finally pumped out, mining began again from the fourteenth level, or 1,060 feet.

New pumps and hoisting machinery were a necessity if they were to continue sinking the shaft. The cost seemed prohibitive – $100,000 plus customs duties of $30,000 – given the company's financial situation. Nevertheless the corporate lawyer, A. J. Cattanach of Toronto, was instructed "to go to Ottawa and try to arrange for getting the duties taken off". His argument was based on the unavailability of similar equipment in Canada.

Head office extended every effort to keep the mine operating. Hadn't the company endured such dire straits before? And hadn't they been saved at the eleventh hour by the second bonanza?

Trethewey carried out an inventory of assets, with instructions to assess everything at its actual value. As a result items considered non-essential were sold during the summer of 1883. These included the scows, small boats, assay equipment, ore bags and even the *Silver Spray*.

Longterm projects were discontinued. For example, work on the shaft on Burnt Island stopped at 162 feet. The idea had been to sink it deep enough to connect with the ninth level on the Islet.

One after another the other locations proved disappointing. Only Mamainse at the eastern end of the lake showed promise. Thomas H. Trethewey had been in charge of developing the property there since 1882 and certain English parties showed serious interest in purchasing it.

Production at Silver Islet mine for 1883 dwindled to a mere $2,010, the result of a worldwide economic depression, yet Trethewey's report sounded hopeful:

> The vein though well defined and carrying quantities of minerals, has not produced the expected amount of silver ...

> It will be remembered that heretofore we have worked for long periods in ground such as described, and finally been rewarded by encountering rich deposits, and there is no reason why we should not expect similar results again.[7]

By now the shaft extended 1,160 feet to the fifteenth level, from which two winzes had been sunk. One of them at 90 feet brought the total depth of the mine to 1,250 feet.[8] Almost a quarter of a mile.

At this point head office saw only two chances of saving the mine – hitting a bonanza or selling the Mamainse property. Since the bonanza hadn't occurred they ordered stringent economy measures for the winter in preparation for the expected sale. Accordingly Trethewey rolled back the payroll to 42 men and confined underground work to the upper portion of the mine. Once more the lower reaches flooded, for the last time as it turned out.

The English parties, for some reason, lost interest in Mamainse and the transaction fell through. In desperation head office mailed a circular to shareholders in mid-January advising of the critical situation and offering as a solution "the sale of Mamainse to the shareholders ratably."[9] Shareholders failed to respond.

At the same time Trethewey informed head office that the *H. B. Tuttle* failed to arrive before freezeup with coal for the winter and that the supply on hand would last only until about March 1, 1884. When the fires went out the engines could no longer power the pumps. The shaft flooded from within, filling to the top for the first time since underground operations began in 1871. The smokestack no longer belched forth its signal that all was well. On March 1 Trethewey cut the payroll to 13 men.

Only a miracle could save the mine now.

PART V
EPILOGUE

CHAPTER 19

AFTERMATH

T he miracle did not happen. Instead a diphtheria epidemic swept Silver Islet mainland in March 1884, claiming the life of John and Catherine Trethewey's daughter, Lena. As soon as circumstances allowed, the community began to disperse.

Some moved to Prince Arthur's Landing, newly incorporated as the town of Port Arthur and booming with construction of the breakwater and the CPR eastward along the north shore. These included the widows Jane McPherson and Hannah Everington, and the families of William Craig, Dennis Higgins, W. C. Mapledoram, Joseph Whalen and Nicholas Marin, formerly captain of the *Silver Spray*. Dr. Lorne C. Campbell became Port Arthur's Medical Officer of Health, but only briefly. He died from an unidentified malady in December 1884 at age 34.

Others gravitated to new silver mines to the southwest, discovered in 1882 and 1883 by Oliver Daunais. Thought to be extensions of the Silver Islet vein, the finds centered at Rabbit Mountain and Silver Mountain.[1] In 1884 both John and Richard Trethewey worked here as mining captains, followed later by Thomas H. Trethewey.

Still others scattered to Houghton and other, more distant mines. The John Strachan family settled in Phoenix, Michigan. John and Fanny Plummer made their home, and their fortune, at the Granite Mountain silver mine in Montana.

Silver Islet closed as a customs port in May 1884 and as a post office in August. John Livingstone relocated to Fort William where he continued with the customs department. James W. Cross remained at Silver Islet as constable and caretaker, resettling his family in the Livingstone home. His liaison with the Silver Islet Consolidated Mining and Lands Company continued through Julian Gifford, a former resident of Silver Islet who returned to New York when the mine closed.

Richard Trethewey kept busy at Silver Islet till the end of August 1884. During his nine years as superintendent the mine produced an estimated $1,085,413 in silver.[2] Closure was caused by the mine's failure to reveal another bonanza, not Trethewey's performance as superintendent. Under his supervision the underground workings attained a depth of 1,250 feet and a maximum width of 1,380 feet at the ninth level; 5,000 feet of cores were bored with the diamond drill; and the inclined shaft was constructed.

He oversaw considerable exploration above ground too. The diamond drill

	Weight in Lbs.	Value per Ton. $ c.	Total Value. $ c.
Under Montreal Mining Co 27,073 3/8		1,646.80	23,115.35
Under New Proprietors, 1870 155,543		1,175.80	92,153.23
Under New Proprietors, 1871 (Newark) 183,453		1,507.64	138,291.88
Under New Proprietors, 1971 (Wyandotte) 778,468 1/2		1,296.48	504,640.13
Lost on propellor "Coborn" 10,000		1,040.00	5,200.00
	1,154,537 7/8	$1,322.44	$763,400.59
Season 1872 . . . . 310,744.02 ozs.			
Season 1873 . . . . 289,763.77 ozs.			
Season 1874 . . . . 250,021.75 ozs.			
Season 1875 . . . . 145,902.50 ozs.			
. . . . 996,432.04 ozs.		=	$1,195,718.45
Produced by stamp mill, 1875, to Nov., 1876 (concentrates). . . . . 136,529.00 ozs			163,835.00
Produced by stoping in upper part of the mine, 1877 . . . . 23,850.00 ozs			28,620.00
Produced from second *bonanza*, 1878. . . . . 721,632.00 ozs			865,958.00
Produced from deposit at 960 ft. level, about 1882. (Mentioned in Mr. Lowe's paper)			30,000.00
Total amounts mentioned in various accounts of the mine as above			$3,047,532.04
Amount unaccounted for above			202,467.96
			3,250,000.00
Total value of silver produced from the commencement to the close of operations, according to Mr. Richard Trethewey			$3,250,000.00

Table 8a.
*Yield in dollars
1868–1884*

SILVER PRODUCTION AT SILVER ISLET

1868	1,000	troy ounces silver
1869	17,950	
1870	70,887	
1871	520,896	
1872	310,744	
1873	289,764	
1874	250,022	
1875	145,903	
1876	124,981	
1877	23,850	
1878	721,632	
1879	50,000	
1880	36,375	
1881	?	
1882	23,256	
1883	1,874	
1884–1921	nil	
1922	16,652	
1869–1922	2,605,786	ounces (81,118kg)

Table 8b.
*Yield in ounces
1868–1922*

EXPORTS OF SILVER ORE FROM 1871 TO 1873

Fiscal Year	Ontario	British Columbia	Total.
1871	$595,261	$	$595,261
1872	1,087,839	803	1,088,6742
1873	1,376,060	(a) 3,320	1,379,380
Total.	$3,059,060	$41,23	$3,063,283

(a) Probably from near Fort Hope

EXPORTS OF SILVER ORE FROM 1873 TO 1886 INCLUSIVE

Year.	Ontario.	Quebec.	New Brunswick	Manitoba.	British Columbia.	Total.
1873	$1,241,598	$	$	$	$2,160	$1,243,758
1874	493,168				300	493,463
1875	472,092				900	472,992
1876	354,178					354,178
1877	33,772	8,626	500			42,848
1878	665,665	50				665,715
1879	154,273					154,273
1880	65,205	3,000				68,205
1881	15,105				10	15,115
1882	6,505	200				6,705
1883	8,620					8,620
1884	13,300					13,300
1885	28,801		117	258		29,176
1886	16,505	(a) 8,000		1,452		25,957
Total.	$3,568,732	$19,876	$617	$1,710	$3,370	$3,594,305

(a) Probably from Thunder Bay District.

worked on Burnt Island, on the mainland and on Shangoina Island. It was here, in the fall of 1878, that the bit broke and couldn't be repaired before winter. The final record of its use is dated January 1880.[3]

The Silver Islet vein was traced a full 9,000 feet, surfacing as it crossed Burnt Island and for 1,800 feet on the mainland. Considerable trenching was carried out as well as blasting four shafts, one 162 feet on Burnt Island and three on the mainland reaching depths of 40 feet, 100 feet and 60 feet. The one furthest inland, called Morgan's Junction, produced ore that assayed at 19 ounces of silver to the ton.

On the mainland, the vein cut through 21 dikes. Silver Islet's offshore dike extends 1200 feet southwest through Pyritic Island to Ship Island and 1600 feet northeast, for a total of 2800 feet. The dike's width at Silver Islet is 350 feet, shrinking to 250 feet by the ninth level and remaining constant to the bottom of the mine.[4]

The vein glistened a brilliant white visible on calm days 20 feet below the surface of the water. Similar veins running northwest and southeast could be seen off Catholic Point, in Camp Bay, on a small island east of Tee Harbour, and near Ship Island.[5] Despite extensive exploration, no vein as rich as Silver Islet's was located.

Silver Islet Landing soon began to look deserted. On Christmas Eve 1871 the company had provided one drink of beer, wine or whisky when the men quit work - early - at four o'clock. Christmas Day saw special dinners in boarding-houses and family dwellings, followed by a skating party on Surprise Lake. But in 1884 Mrs. Cross prepared Christmas dinner for her husband, their seven children and three invited guests, William P. Coo and George Fenn and his mother. They were company employees, the only people still remaining on the Woods Location.

Little by little the equipment dispersed too. Captain John W. Cousins operated the *Silver Spray* in 1884 for its owner James Conmee of Port Arthur. Coincidentally, both men had carried the mail from Pigeon River for a season during the 1870s. The following year Conmee sold the *Silver Spray* to a tug company on the St. Lawrence River. The historic workhorse ran out of Sorel, between Quebec and Montreal, until being destroyed in June 1893.[6]

In 1886 Rabbit Mountain Mine and nearby Beaver Mine bought Silver Islet's ore cars, tracks and other machinery, including the distinctive mill whistle.* That summer the stamp mill at Rabbit Mountain turned out a silver brick, the first one to be produced in the region. For a time it seemed as though the new mines might eclipse Silver Islet. However the value of their total production amounted to only $1,520,000, less than half of Silver Islet's at $3,250,000.[7]

The Silver Islet Consolidated Mining and Lands Company launched an $80,000 lawsuit against Hannah of Cleveland, owners of the *H. B. Tuttle*, for damages resulting from non-delivery of the coal. This and other claims and counterclaims involving the company appeared before United States and Canadian courts for a number of years. As a result of one of them, all lands

* The mill whistle found its final usefulness on the steamship *Alberta*, and was scrapped with the ship.

belonging to the company were sold by auction September 19, 1888 in New York. The American Exchange National Bank acquired the property for $5,000.[8]

On July 10, 1890 trustees John J. Marvin and Henry S. Sibley released an official statement that included the following sentence:

> When work ceased at Silver Islet in February 1884 (owing to the non-arrival of coal, unfortunately shipped in charge of an intemperate captain in the fall of 1883), the appearance of the vein in that mine was in every respect encouraging.[9]

The statement was a preliminary response to the Sherman Silver Purchase Act passed four days later. This legislation required the United States Treasury to buy 4,500,000 ounces of silver every month. In these circumstances it seemed the mine might open again.

The local press also speculated that Silver Islet would be "put in condition for use". Thomas H. Trethewey was hired to supervise exploration of Mamainse, among other locations, as well as Edward Island at the mouth of Black Bay. Assayer W. M. Courtis compared ore from Edward Island with that from Silver Islet. It seemed as though a silver mine would become a reality, if not at Silver Islet then on Edward Island.

At the critical moment a Canadian court placed a judgment of more than $100,000 against the Silver Islet Consolidated Mining and Lands Company. As a result the Woods Location, including water lots, was sold at auction in Port Arthur in October 1891.[10] Only four people attended the sale, among them Thomas H. Trethewey and a relative of A. H. Sibley, Frederick T. Sibley. The latter paid $1,860 for the property and promptly turned the title over to trustees Marvin and Henry S. Sibley.

By this time the Sherman Silver Purchase Act was having a negative effect. The Treasury's policy of issuing new currency to buy the silver led to its depreciation. Thomas H. Trethewey was sent to Mamainse with a diamond drill in December 1891 to explore for copper instead.

During the summer of 1892 the falling price of silver closed most of the mines in the Rabbit Mountain and Silver Mountain region. That fall the Silver Islet company opted to pour its resources into copper. Thomas H. Trethewey went to Mamainse as superintendent with a complete mining outfit.[11] Shortly thereafter the failure of the Philadelphia & Reading Railroad set off a spiral that ended with the crash of the Wall Street stock market in July 1893. The depression of the 1890s had begun.

The economy recovered slowly as the twentieth century dawned. Hopes of Silver Islet reopening dimmed, however, with development of the silver find at Cobalt, Ontario. In 1905, its third year of operation, this remarkable mine yielded $5,401,766, surpassing in a single season the total production of its famous predecessor.

Silver Islet structures continued to disappear. Woodside Brothers, a machine shop in Port Arthur, bought the stamp mill machinery in 1906. On May 15, 1920, a fire on Silver Islet destroyed the engine house, both shafthouses, and the office.[12] Subsequently parts of the battered cribbing collapsed, spilling the remaining buildings and rocks into the lake.

But there was one other chance to revive the mine. Some of the property had come to the Cross family early in 1919 and one of the sons, Julian G. Cross, "picked tailings from the Silver Islet mine and raised $800".[13] Jule, as he was called, graduated from Queen's University in 1916 as a geologist. He is best known as the discoverer of iron ore under Steep Rock Lake, near Atikokan.

The price of silver reached a record high of $1.11 an ounce in 1919.[14] The following spring the Islet Exploration Company of Duluth took an option on the mine and the underwater property. Activity continued for 2 1/2 years under mining engineer D. C. Peacock and R. C. Jamison. It came as a disappointment that the price of silver fell to 63 cents an ounce during this period, also that ice didn't form strong enough to carry the weight of a diamond drill.

The mine was dewatered each summer for three years. A certain amount of sampling on the first level in 1920 justified extensive work on the fourth level in 1921. A drift 127 feet long was blasted in a southwesterly direction, followed by 1,000 feet of borings with a diamond drill both underground and from the Islet's surface. The holes hit two veins and plenty of water, but no silver. Unwanted rock was dropped down the inclined shaft; the rest was brought to the surface.

The project began with great hoopla. Starting the engine was the Hon. Harry Mills, the first Ontario Cabinet member to represent a Thunder Bay riding. Captain Cross hoisted the old Union Jack from former times. The press reported that a log structure "still intact with walls in good condition" remained on the Islet, having withstood wind and weather for half a century.

A Duluth firm worked the mine during the early 1920s.

The company finished exploration in 1922 by removing ore from the ceiling of the mine. Ore recovered yielded 16,652 ounces of silver worth $10,971, while expenses totalled $84,000.[15]

Despite public knowledge of this loss, the old mine continued to attract investors. The property was optioned in 1975 by Q. C. Explorations Limited, owned by Tom Gledhill of Toronto. This firm carried out extensive underwater exploration, including the fault line between the Islet and the mainland and rock samples from the collapsed cribs around the Islet. As a result Q. C. Explorations Limited acquired the property in 1984 and installed a mill in the city of Thunder Bay to concentrate rock dredged from around the Islet. The resulting concentrates brought in a disappointing $10,000 and the mill closed.[16]

CHAPTER 20
NOSTALGIA THAT LINGERS

At first glance Silver Islet looks like a giant bald head with a few straggly hairs growing on top. No trace of the mine remains except underwater, where the distinctive outline of the cribbing is clearly visible to those who know it's there. More difficult to spot are the shafts. They can be seen clearly only on bright days, black holes undulating beneath sun-dappled swells, mysterious and foreboding.

The mine has inspired tales, many of them tall, ever since the beginning. Highgrading was a popular theme. One story is that a group of miners secreted three barrels of silver nuggets in a cave that opened into the shaft, but failed to return for them before the mine flooded. Another tale describes how miners brought rich ore to the surface and tied it to a log, then set the log adrift to be retrieved later.

Maude Livingstone personified imaginative possibilities as revealed by Captain Cross:

> He will tell you that sometimes, when the air is full of light and when the wind sleeps and the placid water reflects the great blue bowl of heaven, the surface of the lake will suddenly heave in long, low swells, and then smooth out again; then as from the depths of the earth come low rumbling sounds, muffled and indistinct like a far-off cannonade.[1]

Captain Cross himself was featured on the cover of Anna G. Young's book *Off Watch: Today and Yesterday on the Great Lakes*, standing on the dock.

The mainland is a living museum. A sturdy dock still juts from the company store, a weathered three-story structure newly refurbished as a general store and tea room by the Lorne Saxberg family. Well-kept homes line the Avenue. Some of them are new, but many date back to the mining era.

There's the imposing Livingstone/Cross residence and Captain Marin's quaint cottage of squared timbers with its souvenir shop. There's the hotel, really two frame buildings joined together, and the schoolhouse bereft of its belfry. One after another they come into view, the newer buildings blending easily with the original miners' homes in a typical Canadian summer colony.

Ross Matthews recorded in his memoirs a story of the first family to camp at Silver Islet, as told by his Aunt Martha Dickinson:

'It was the time your Aunt Christine got the Black Diphtheria and that must have been about 1891'...

Christine had kissed Aunt Martha's own little sister Nancy through the back fence of their adjoining properties, presumably some time before she turned black. Nancy of course came down with Diphtheria too, and because it was the dreaded black kind the M. O. H. had to double the quarantine period to six weeks instead of the customary three. This would apply even to those members of the family who were considering moving to a hotel.

It looked like a long siege for both families, so Mr. Dickinson, who knew Captain Cross from their comradeship in that fraternal organization known as the Protestant Protective Association or Orangemen, said to my grandfather Munro "Why don't we take our families over to Silver Islet? We can live in one of those empty miners' houses on the mainland. Captain Cross won't mind. There will be no quarantine regulations over there and our children will have all outdoors to play in rather than the lot of us being impounded behind four walls."

It seemed like a wonderful idea. Captain Maloney, who had fishing nets out that way, took a message over to Captain Cross and on his next trip the Dickinsons, as the first contingent of the invading force, set out with their barrels of flour, their bedding and a cow.

Captain Cross was there to greet them alright, with a pike pole to hold off the little fishing tug, the "Gracie". It wasn't a wonderful idea to him. None of his family had had Diphtheria and they weren't going to if he could help it. Captain Maloney managed to get one of the tug's heavy rope hawsers around the mooring post while Mr. Dickinson and Captain Cross shouted at each other to be reasonable.

There was quite a swell in the channel. What with a bit of spray to cool one's tempers and the creak of the Gracie's fender against the dock it would have been a noisy business. Mr. Dickinson and the Captain finally adjourned a little way to where they could hear each other and Captain Maloney quietly got the Dickinsons and their baggage on to the dock. Shouting that he had nets to lift, but that he would be back before dark, and if they hadn't settled it by then he'd take them all back home, Captain Maloney cast off and was away down the channel. The Dickinsons were sitting on their belongings with Captain Cross still adamant, when Mrs. Cross came down to see what it was all about.

Mrs. Cross was a kind and deeply religious woman who could not stand the sort of ruckus that was in the making between friends. If it was to be the Will of God there was nothing she would want to do about it. Captain Cross bowed graciously to the intercession of his wife. "You better take the Office", he said. "It's the only house with the windows in."

They took the Office and moved in. By noon, of course, both families were mixed up all over the Islet. Fortunately by the Will of God none of the Cross family got Diphtheria. Captain Maloney brought my grandfather and his family on his next trip.

They had a wonderful summer, the first of many more at Silver Islet.[2]

Just after the turn of the century Captain Cross became a sort of booking agent for the deserted dwellings. At first people arranged for their own transportation, but by 1908 the steamship *Doric* was scheduling three trips weekly between Silver Islet mainland and the newly designated cities of Port Arthur and Fort William, collectively called the Lakehead.

The Cross family opened the store so that campers could buy supplies on site. Before the summer ended most of the homes sported names such as Onawango, Kamp Kill Kare, Sleepy Hollow, Happy Go Lucky, Steprite Inn, and Wide Awake. The President's mansion remained unnamed, although like the other buildings it housed more than one family in a season and often several at the same time, along with guests.

The front doorpost of Frue's home had Burry Worry Lodge emblazoned on it. Sandy Beach was a favourite gathering place for young people. The night scene in 1908 enchanted a young reporter:

The glow of many big bon fires [sic] light up the shores of the camping ground. On the water the boats move back and forth illuminated with lanterns, and the pale radiance of the moon marks a silver pathway across the wider water.

To the merry groups clustered around the camp fires, roasting potatoes and telling stories, there floats the snatches of music wooed from mandolin or banjo.[3]

Was it only 30 years before that a similar scene was being acted out on Burnt Island? The difference was in the social status enjoyed by the mine's white-collar employees. A former resident recalled the Gifford sisters, one of whom eventually married Henry S. Sibley:

As a small girl [Mrs. Friday] lived, with her parents, next door to the home of the Giffords of New York. "They were toney people", she says, and the daughters used to walk up and down the Avenue with fascinators [head scarves] of fine lace on their heads and carrying walking canes tied with bright ribbon. One day Mrs. Friday's Mother found her little daughter in the kitchen, with a curtain on her head, trying to tie some ribbon onto an old stick, to emulate the much-envied Misses Gifford.[4]

Woodside Brothers of Port Arthur bought the stamp mill machinery in 1906. By 1913 the smokestack had tumbled to the ground.

The attitudes of the summer colony were more casual.

The mainland offered much more than a spectacular setting and everchanging view. There was the decrepit stamp mill, tumbling down a little more each year; the jail, its cell doors creaking eerily on massive hinges; the Catholic Church with its elevated widow's walk. These structures and others captured the imagination and resulted in endless stories and flights of fancy.

John McPherson, son of Alex and Jane McPherson, told of a ghost dressed in white who lived in the assay office. He saw her on the dock, but others report seeing her in the stamp mill.[5]

Then there was the so-called Irish Castle challenging climbers of all ages. This sheer rock rose so close to the shoreline that only the Avenue could pass. And there was Surprise Lake, somewhat protected from the open winds of the big lake, offering an inland arena for swimmers, boaters and picnickers. Rumour had it that sea monsters lurked in its depths, a tale originating with the giant sturgeon sometimes caught by fishermen. And there was the Sea Lion jutting 50 feet into Lake Superior. Everyone felt like walking along his tawny back at least once, or guiding a boat through the space between his head and forepaws.

The spot became so popular as a summer resort that in 1910 a local group formed a company to purchase the shoreline between the Sea Lion and Camp Bay, including Burnt Island. The Lake Coast Trading Company not only subdivided the tract into lots, it also arranged for regular steamboat transportation from the Lakehead. For the first time the legal machinery was in place so that individuals could gain title to property on the Woods Location.

The developers called the mainland Silver Islet "as it was the most convenient and accessible point from which to operate the Islet itself during the actual mining work."[6] This popular if inaccurate name has survived the test of time. Thankfully some of the other plans failed to materialize. They include turning the shoreline into "Fort William's Coney Island" complete with "a Roller Coaster,

The Sea Lion in Perry's Bay is a favourite attraction. Its geology is similar to the hard diabase dike that forms Silver Islet.

Loop the Loop, Shute the Shutes, Miniature railway, Figure Eight and other such attractions."

Instead the summer colony developed as a holiday retreat for residents of the Lakehead and as a destination for sightseers and picnickers. In 1912 local Boy Scouts pitched 16 or more tents at Silver Islet for their first campout. The following year photographer J. F. Cooke published contemporary scenes in an attractive 20-page booklet titled *Souvenir of Silver Islet, Port Arthur and Fort William's Healthful Summer Resort.* A summer post office operated from 1914 until 1943. Once again the harbour bustled with activity, steamships like the 600-passenger sidewheeler *Forest City* travelling to and fro on a regular basis bringing excursion parties as well as mail and supplies.

Excursions to Silver Islet were not a new idea. Various groups had sponsored mass picnics to Silver Islet as early as the 1890s. In 1893, for example, the Lakehead's Presbyterian and Methodist churches jointly chartered the side-wheeler *Cambria* for a day trip. Five hundred men, women and children attended. The passenger steamer era continued with ships like the *Islet Prince*, but finally gave way to the automobile. The *Keewatin* was the last steamer; she made her final run in the mid-1960s.

Construction of a road in 1931 offered yearround accessibility for the first time. That fall Ernest J. Cross, a son of Captain Cross, drove the length of Sibley Peninsula to Silver Islet over the new road. He was the first to do so. As the road improved, more vehicles began using it.

Today Highway 587 links Silver Islet with Highway 11-17 at the base of Sibley Peninsula, near Pass Lake. The community of the same name began as a Danish settlement, the first immigrants taking up homesteads in 1924 in both Sibley township and neighbouring McTavish township.[7]

The rest of Highway 587 threads its way through *Sibley Provincial Park,** with

*Renamed Sleeping Giant Provincial Park.

park facilities accessible at several entry points. The park was designated in 1936 as a result of lobbying by the Port Arthur Chamber of Commerce. Park status was formalized in 1944, an entity which became a natural environment park in 1967 under the Ontario Provincial Park Classification System.[8] A wildlife sighting during the winding drive to Silver Islet is highly likely, and entering the park itself virtually guarantees it.

Sibley Provincial Park covers most of Sibley township and the Woods Location except for the northeast corner of the township, the federal lighthouse reserve on Thunder Cape and the Silver Islet subdivision of 1910. The park's significant features include the Brohm archaeological site near Pass Lake, numerous orchid sites, the Sleeping Giant and Silver Islet cemetery.

The cemetery is a quaint and crumbling legacy from the past. Picket fences surround each plot, their cornerposts as weatherbeaten as the pickets. Light green lichen in filmy strands hang from them and from the wooden headstones inside the enclosures. A spirit house over an Ojibway grave is the best preserved of all. Names and dates lovingly carved in wood so long ago are now illegible, for the most part. So far 61 depressions and/or graves have been identified.[9]

Silver Islet became a popular destination for day excursions before the First World War.

There are three stone markers, two for Ketty Ann McLean and one carved with the words "Erected by a grateful friend To the memory of Anne Martin. Died May 6th, 1882". Winnifred Philpott wrote about her in a photograph album:

Mrs. Martin was an Englishwoman, who, when a young girl, came to Canada with her infant son. Her husband had received a Twenty year sentence in Newgate Prison, London, for killing a companion in a brawl, and she had decided that she could, by industry and saving, prepare to give him a fresh start in a new world by the time he had served his sentence. She became house-keeper to Major Sibley, the President of S.I. Mine, but just when nineteen

Names on the cemetery's wooden markers are barely legible today.

years had passed, she died. Her wishes that the son carry out her plans were observed, and, with the help and good-wishes of the community, he was sent on his way to England, intending to bring his father back with him to Canada. But from the day of his departure no word was heard from him.[10]

The potential of the Silver Islet story has inspired several local authors. The first of these was Maude Livingstone. Fort William's *Daily Times Journal* published her memoir April 17, 1908 under the title "Silver Islet: The Romance of a Lost Mine". Janey Livingstone expanded on her sister's article after the First World War, adding photographs and a plan of the mine, and published it in a 24-page pamphlet. *Historic Silver Islet: The Story of a Drowned Mine* sold for 75 cents, a fundraising project of the Great War Veterans Association.

The sisters never married. They lived together in the family home in Fort William, earning a precarious living teaching art and giving music lessons. Playwright Laurent Goulet dramatized their struggle with poverty in a play called "The Livingstone Sisters", produced by Cambrian Players during the early 1980s.

Encouraged by the response, Goulet scripted a second play based on events at Silver Islet during its heyday. "Madeleine" was produced by Magnus Theatre and published in 1982 by Playwrights Canada. Elizabeth Kouhi also chose Silver Islet's glory days as a literary setting. Queenston House of Winnipeg published her children's novel *Sarah Jane of Silver Islet* in 1983.

Historical accounts include Gertrude Dyke's pamphlet *Historic Silver Islet* and Helen Moore Strickland's *Silver Under the Sea*, both released in 1979. The film "Rise and Fall of Silver Islet" premièred in Thunder Bay on April 24, 1986, sponsored by the National Film Board. Local bard Bill Houston composed and performed the music for this 24½ minute documentary scripted by Robert

Sandler and produced by Peter Elliott of Toronto. In 1993 New Creations Theatre produced a play for school children entitled "The Tree Spirit of Silver Islet", written by Lila Cano and Janis Swanson, with music by Rodney Brown. Lenni Albanese starred as the tree spirit Spriggan, and Janis Swanson played the roles of six pioneers including Macfarlane, Frue, and Mrs. Trethewey. It seems as though Silver Islet is casting its spell over a wider audience than ever before.

The continuing fascination lies not in Silver Islet's status as Canada's first successful mine and first silver producer, nor even in the richness of the lode, although this was considered extraordinary at the time. No, the secret is in its offshore location.

What other mineshaft is located beneath the world's largest freshwater lake? What other mining company housed its workers on a fortified island? Or traced the vein with deep sea diving equipment?

Consider the odds. Discovery of the vein virtually underwater was a fluke, a lucky break. Development of a frontier mine on a tiny toehold exposed to the full sweep of Lake Superior called for unusual courage and know-how. Construction of the incredible rampart required to support the surface structures and bring the mine into production marked an engineering feat of epic proportions.

Silver Islet was indeed a most improbable mine.

BIBLIOGRAPHY

Selected Books

Arthur, Elizabeth. *Thunder Bay District 1821-1892: A Collection of Documents.* Toronto: Champlain Society, 1973 .

Bertrand, J. P. *Highway of Destiny: An Epic Story of Canadian Development.* New York: Vantage, 1959.

Nelles, H. V. *The Politics of Development: Forests, Mines and Hydro-Electric Power in Ontario 1849-1941.* Toronto: Macmillan, 1974.

Newell, Dianne. *Technology on the Frontier: Mining in Old Ontario.* Vancouver: University of British Columbia Press, 1986.

Piper, W. S. *The Eagle of Thunder Cape.* New York: Knickerbocker, 1924.

Reid, Dorothy M. *Tales of Nanabozho.* Toronto: Oxford University Press, 1963.

Roland, A. W. *Algoma West: Its Mines, Scenery and Industrial Resources.* Toronto, 1887.

Roland, A. W. *Port Arthur Illustrated.* Winnipeg, 1889.

Rowe, John. *The Hard Rock Men: Cornish Immigrants and the North American Mining Frontier.* England: University of Liverpool Press, 1974.

Stafford, Sara. *The Discovery of the Five Great Lakes.* Toronto: Hunter-Ross, 1910.

Zaslow, Morris. *Reading The Rocks: The Story of the Geological Survey of Canada 1842-1972.* Toronto: Macmillan, 1975.

Printed Reports

Canada. Geological Survey. *Report of Progress.* Coste, E. "Statistical Report on the Production, Value, Exports and Imports of Minerals in Canada during the Year 1886 and Previous Years", (1887): 73S-75S.

Ingall, E. D. "Report on Mines and Mining on Lake Superior. Part I. A History and General Condition of the Region", 1887-88, (new series), volume 3, part 2, (1888).

Robb, C. "Records of Mines and Mineral Statistics..", "Table 1-Province of Ontario", (1872): 147.

Canada. Geological Survey. Tanton, T. L. *Fort William and Port Arthur, and Thunder Cape Map-Areas, Thunder Bay District, Ontario,* Memoir 167, (1931).

Canada. *Sessional Papers.* Logan, W. E. "Report of Progress for the Year 1846-47", Appendix (C), (n.p., 1847), 15 pages.

Canada. *Statutes.*

Frue, W. B. "Brief Sketch of Silver Islet", supplement to Silver Mining Company of Silver Islet, *Annual Report*, (New York, 1874). Reprinted in *Thunder Bay Sentinel*, August 5, 12, 19, 1875.

McKellar, Peter. *Mining on the North Shore, Lake Superior.* (1874), 26 pages.

Mohide, T. P. *Silver.* Ontario Mineral Policy Background Paper No. 20, (Toronto, 1985).

Montreal Mining Company. *Annual Reports.* 1846, 1851 through 1855, 1859.

Ontario. Bureau of Mines. *Annual Report.* Blue, A. "The Story of Silver Islet", volume 6, (1897): 125-158.

> Bowen, N. L. "Silver in Thunder Bay District", volume 20, part 1, (1911): 119-132.

> Miller, W. G. "Lake Superior Silver Deposits", volume 19, part 2, (1910): 197-210.

Ontario. Department of Mines. *Annual Report.* Parsons, A. L. "Silver Islet Mine", volume 30, part 4, (1921): 34-38.

Ontario. *Sessional Papers.* McKellar, Peter. "Silver", No. 72, (1895): 237-239.

Ontario. *Statutes.*

Report of the Royal Commission on the Mineral Resources of Ontario and Measures for Their Development, (Toronto, 1890).

Sibley, A. H. *Report on Mining on the North Shore of Lake Superior*, by A. H. Sibley, President of Silver Islet Company, (n.p., 1873).

Sibley Provincial Park, Master Plan, (Ontario, Ministry of Natural Resources, 1980).

Silver Islet Consolidated Mining and Lands Company. *Annual Report*, (New York, 1879 and 1884)

Silver Islet Employees Benefit Society. *Constitution and By-Laws*, (1880).

Silver Mining Company of Silver Islet. *Annual Report*, (New York, 1874).

Selected articles, booklets and theses

Arthur, Elizabeth. "The Founding Father" [Peter McKellar]. Thunder Bay Historical Museum Society [hereafter TBHMS], *Papers & Records 1983*: 10-22.

Canadian Champion and County of Halton Intelligencer, (Milton, Ontario). "Press Excursion", 23 July 1868.

Courtis, W. M. "The Wyandotte Silver Smelting and Refining Works". *Transactions of the American Institute of Mining Engineers*, 2, (1873-74): 89-101.

Coyne, J. H. "A Week on Lake Superior". TBHS, *Papers of 1926-27*: 130-132. Reprinted from *St. Thomas Journal*, (1871).

Cross, Brenda. "Silver Islet Inhabitants: 1868-1944". *Past Tents*, (newsletter of Thunder Bay District Branch, Ontario Genealogical Society), May 1984 through May 1986.

Cross, Margaret. "Famed Silver Islet had Brief but Spectacular History". *Daily Times Journal*, (Fort William, Ontario), 23 June 1934.

Cuthbertson, George A. "Montreal Mining Company's Men Surveying the Joseph Woods Location....". *Canadian Mining Journal*, (1939): 353-354.

Daily Mining Gazette, (Houghton, Michigan). "Frue's Silver Islet Days are Relived by his Hancock Niece", 1 February 1964; "Frue House, A Shrine to 'World's Greatest Silver Mine Engineer'", 26 August 1967.

Daily Times Journal, (Fort William, Ontario). "Silver Islet Summer Resort", 15 August 1908; "Fire Destroys Historic House at Silver Islet", 24 March 1930; "John McPherson Lifts Curtain on Early Days Here", 14 April 1934 .

Evening Chronicle, (Port Arthur, Ontario). "How Nanna Bijou wrested back Hidden Treasure from Man's Ruthless Hand", 21 May 1910.

Forster, John H. "The History of the Settlement of Silver Islet on the North Shore of Lake Superior". Typescript credited to *Michigan Pioneer and Historical Collections*, 14, (rev. ed., 1889).

French, William A. "Silver Mining in the Thunder Bay Region 1845-1891: An Fxamination of its Economic Viability". Thesis, Lakehead University, Geography Department, 1976.

Haste, Richard A. "The Lost Mine of Silver Islet" in TBHS, *Papers of 1926-27*: 36-43. Reprinted from *Dearborn Independent*.

Herald, (Duluth, Minnesota). "Silver Islet, Its Value and Location", 19 June 1875. Reprinted from *Marquette Journal*.

Jestin, W.J. "Provincial Policy and the Development of the Metallic Mining Industry in Northern Ontario, 1845-1920". Thesis, University of Toronto, 1977.

Lankton, Larry D. "Paternalism and Social Control in the Lake Superior Copper Mines, 1845-1913". *Upper Midwest History*, 5, (1985): 1-17.

Livingstone, Christina Maude. "Silver Islet: The Romance of a Lost Mine". *Daily Times Journal*, (Fort William, Ontario), 17 April 1908.

Livingstone, Janey C. *Historic Silver Islet: The Story of a Drowned Mine*. (Fort William, c1919), 24 pages.

Lowe, F. A. "The Silver Islet mine and its present developments". *Engineering and Mining Journal*, 34, (1882): 320-323.

Lowe, F. A. "Treatment of Low-Grade Silver Ores at the Silver Islet Mill". *Engineering and Mining Journal*, 32, (1881): 251-253.

McDermott, Walter. "The Frue Concentrator". *Transactions of the American Institute of Mining Engineers*, 3, (1874-75): 357-360.

McDermott, Walter. "The Silver Islet Vein, Lake Superior". *Canadian Mining Journal*, 30, (1909): 135-138. Reprinted in *Thunder Bay Sentinel*, 28 October 1875.

Macfarlane, Thomas. "On the Geology and Silver Ore of Woods Location, Thunder Cape, Lake Superior". *The Canadian Naturalist*, 4, (1869): 37-48, 459-463.

Macfarlane, Thomas. "Silver Islet". *Transactions of the American Institute of Mining Engineers*, 8, (1879-80): 226-253. Extracts published in W. J. Hamilton, "Silver Islet: Extracts from a paper read by Thomas Macfarlane ... at a Montreal meeting, September, 1879". TBHS, *Papers of 1911-12*: 31-42.

McKanday, George. "A Short Life, A Long Memory". *Globe and Mail*, 11 January 1963.

McKellar, Peter. "Early Mining". TBHS, *Papers of 1918*: 15-17.

McKellar, Peter. "The Otter Head Tin Swindle". TBHS, *Papers of 1912-13*: 11-13.

Milwaukee Journal, "Legend of Nanbijou", 10 December 1961.

Moore, Watson W. "Legends of the Sleeping Giant". TBHS, *Papers of 1924-25*: 26-27. Reprinted from *Thunder Bay Sentinel*, 9 January 1889, and copied by it from *Puget Sound Magazine*.

Newell, Dianne. "Silver mining in the Thunder Bay District, 1865-1885". TBHMS, *Papers & Records 1985*: 28-45 .

Rowe, R. C. "The Discovery of Silver Islet: Being Extracts from the diary of Thomas Macfarlane". *Canadian Mining Journal*, (1936): 222-227; 266-271.

Scott, Beryl H. "Silver Islet Landing". *Canadian Geocraphical Journal*, (March 1956): 126-131.

Scott, Beryl H. "The Story of Silver Islet". *Ontario History*, 46, (Summer 1957): 125-137.

Sladen, G. "Side Trip to Silver Islet". *Ontario Homes and Living*, (May 1966): 9-11.

Smyk, Mark C. "A Comparative Study of Silver Occurrences, Island Belt Silver Region, Thunder Bay District, Ontario". Thesis, Lakehead University, Geology Department, 1984.

Souvenir of Silver Islet, Port Arthur and Fort William's Healthful Summer Resort, (Port Arthur, 1913), 20 pages.

Stiff, John. "Silver Islet, Cursed Bonanza". *Canadian Geographical Journal*, (August 1973): 14-19.

Swift, Ivan. "Ne-Naw-Bo-Zhoo - Mighty Man" in TBHS, Papers of 1926-27: 56-59. Reprinted from *Dearborn Independent*.

Tanton, T. L. "Silver Islet and Vicinity, Thunder Bay District, Ontario". *Transactions of the Canadian Mining Institute*, 23, (1920): 402-418.

Thompson, John. "Silver Islet". *Horizon Canada, 5*, (Number 58): 1388-1392.

Thunder Bay Sentinel, (Port Arthur, Ontario). "Visit to Silver Islet", 28 October 1875; "The Governor General's Visit", 28 July 1881.

"Unveiling of Historic Plaques" in TBHS, *Papers of 1967*: 23-26.

Wilkins, Charles. "Silver Islet". *Cottage Life*, (March 1994): 42-51

Wilson, Wendell E. "Silver Islet". *The Mineralogical Record*, 17, (January-February 1986): 49-60.

Documents

Montreal.

McGill University, Rare Books Library.
    Montreal Mining Company, *Annual Report*, 1846.
    Thomas Macfarlane Papers.

Ottawa.

Public Archives of Canada.
    Algoma Silver Mining Company Papers.
    T. A. Keefer Papers.
    Winnifred Philpott Papers.

St. Jérôme.

Jesuit Archives.
    Father Baxter's Notes.

Thunder Bay.

Bob Faithfull Collection.
>Documents and photographs.

Brodie Resource Library, Reference Department.
>Letters and Reports on Silver Islet Mine.
>Frue Letterbook [typescript].

Lakehead University Library Archives.
>Silver Islet Collection, archive 38.
>Matthews, Ross, "Oft in the Stilly Night", (n.d.).

Municipality of Shuniah.
>Council Minute Books.

Resident Geologist's Office.
>Frue Letterbook [typescript].
>Newspaper clippings.
>Mines file.
>Cross, J. G. "Silver in Thunder Bay District with Special Reference to Silver Islet mine and the Edwards Island Silver Prospect", (1961).
>Roberts, Hugh M. "Memorandum on an Examination of Silver Islet", (1920).

St. Andrew's Rectory.
>Official Register, volume 1B.
>Bertrand, J. P. "Pioneers of the Cross in Northwestern Ontario", (1952).

Thunder Bay Historical Museum Society.
>Frue Letterbook [typescript].
>Invoice Books.
>Contracts Book.
>Diamond Drill Record.
>Folkes, P., comp. "Navigation on the Great Lakes 1871: A collection of selected Marine News from the Toronto *Globe* May 12 - December 30, 1871", (1971).

Toronto.

Archives of Ontario.
>Attorney General Records.
>Cross Family Papers [microfilm].
>St. John the Evangelist Parish Registers [microfilm].

Metropolitan Toronto Library.
>Journal of Sir William Logan, 1846.
>Montreal Mining Company, *Annual Reports*.

ENDNOTES

Part I
Prologue

Chapter 1
An Unusual Setting (pages 10-12)

1. J. H. Coyne, "A Week on Lake Superior", Thunder Bay Historical Society [hereafter TBHS], *Papers of 1926-27*, 132. Reprinted from *St. Thomas Journal*, (1871). For a contemporary description of a thunderstorm, see C. M. Vickers, "Thunder Bay and the Kaministiquia Half a century Ago. A Letter from Catherine Moodie Vickers to her Mother, Susanna Moodie, Toronto, Sunday, August 31st, 1873", TBHS, *Papers of 1924-25*, pp. 52-58.

Chapter 2
Copper and Silver (pages 13-17)

1. W. E. Logan, "Report of Progress of the Geological Survey for 1843" as reprinted in E. D. Ingall, "Report on Mines and Mining on Lake Superior", Canada, Geological Survey, *Annual Report*, 1887-8, (new series), v. 3, pt. 2, p. 9H [*hereafter Ingall's Report (1888)*].

2. Joseph Woods was a son of James Woods, solicitor for Lord Selkirk's settlement at Baldoon. He saw action on the Detroit frontier during the Rebellion of 1837 as a lieutenant-colonel in the militia. Elected to the first union parliament in 1841, Woods represented Kent county as a Tory until 1848. He never married.

3. For a firsthand account, see *Journal of Sir William Logan*, 1846, held by Metropolitan Toronto Library.

4. W. E. Logan, "Report of Progress for the Year 1846-47", Canada, Legislative Assembly, *Appendix to the Journals*, Appendix (C), 1847, 12th page.

5. *Ibid.*, 8th page. Logan's report reads:

... bluish slates with their associated volcanic layers, compose the whole of the country, islands and mainland, between Pigeon River and Fort William.

Eastward on the main front of the lake, it constitutes Pie Island, and the promontory of Thunder Cape, reaching to a point about six miles to the eastward of its extremity, where a transverse dislocation lets down the succeeding formation at least 1,300 feet.

6. Thunder Bay Historical Museum Society, Letters to J. McKenzie, B4/5/13-19; Forrest Shepherd, 18 May 1846. Reprinted in TBHS, *Papers of 1967*, p. 7.

7. McGill University, Rare Books Library; *Report of the Montreal Mining Company*, (Montreal, 1846), p. 19.

8. John Rowe, *The Hard Rock Men: Cornish Immigration and the North American Frontier*, (England: University of Liverpool Press, 1974), Appendix II, "Shipments of Rough Copper from Lake Superior 1845-61", p. 298.

9. E. B. Borron, "Report of the Mining Inspector", Ontario, Department of Crown Lands, *Report*, 1870; also his testimony in Ontario, *Report of the Royal Commission on the Mineral Resources of Ontario and Measures for Their Development*, (Toronto, 1890), p. 194.

10. For a study of Peter McKellar, the man and the myth, see Elizabeth Arthur, "The Founding Father", Thunder Bay Historical Museum Society [*hereafter TBHMS*], *Papers & Records 1983*, pp. 10-22; for family information see E. Marion Henderson, *The McKellar Story: McKellar Pioneers in Lake Superior's Mineral Country, 1839-1929*, (Thunder Bay, McKellar General Hospital Auxiliary, 1981).

11. Rowe, *The Hard Rock Men*, p. 298.

12. J. P. Bertrand, *Highway of Destiny: An Epic Story Of Canadian Development*, (New York, Vantage, 1959), pp. 188-9.

Part II
Underwater, Of All Places

Chapter 3
A Promising Vein (pages 22-25)

1. Thomas Macfarlane, "On the Geology and Silver Ore of Woods Location, Thunder Cape, Lake Superior", *The Canadian Naturalist*, 4, (1869), p. 45 [*hereafter, Macfarlane, "On the Geology" (1869)*].

2. Thomas Macfarlane, "Silver Islet", *Transactions Of The American Institute Of Mining Engineers*, 8, (1880), p. 231 [*hereafter, Macfarlane, "Silver Islet" (1880)*].

3. "Press Excursion", *Canadian Champion and County of Halton Intelligencer*, (Milton, Ontario), 23 July 1868.

Chapter 4
All Hands to Silver Islet (pages 26-29)

1. Macfarlane, "Silver Islet" (1880), p. 243. Subsequent production figures come from pages 243-52 unless specified otherwise.

2. National Archives of Canada [*hereafter NAC*], Hudson's Bay Company Records, B-134-c; R. Crawford to J. Clouston, 19 January 1869 .

3. R. C. Rowe, "The Discovery of Silver Islet: Being Extracts from the diary of Thomas Macfarlane", *Canadian Mining Journal*, (1936), p. 227.

4. *Ibid.*, p. 269.

5. Macfarlane, "On the Geology" (1869), p. 462.

6. Peter McKellar, *Mining on the North Shore, Lake Superior*, (1874), p. 8.

Chapter 5
Fishing Through the Ice for Ore (pages 30-33)

1. *Dictionary of Canadian Biography*, v. 11, p. 781; see also John Thompson, "Silver Islet", *Horizon Canada*, 5, (Number 58), p. 1389.

2. A. H. Sibley, *Report on Mining on the North Shore of Lake Superior, by A. H. Sibley, President of the Silver Islet Mining Company*, (1873), n. p. [*hereafter, Sibley's Report (1873)*].

3. For a full account of the fire see B. Petersen, "The Great Fire of 1870", TBHMS, *Papers & Records 1984*, pp. 8-18 .

4. Great Britain, Parliament, *Correspondence Relative to the Recent Expedition to the Red River Settlement With Journal of Operations*, (London, 1871), p. 43.

5. Archibald Blue, "The Story of Silver Islet", Ontario, Bureau of Mines, *Annual Report*, 1896, v. 6, (1897), p. 141 [*hereafter, Blue's Report (1897)*].

Part III
A Company Town, A Working Mine

Chapter 6
Fifty-eight Immigrants (pages 38-40)

1. John H. Forster, "The History of the Settlement of Silver Islet on the North Shore of Lake Superior", typescript credited to *Michigan Pioneer & Historical Collections*, v. 14, (rev. ed. 1889), pp. 3-6. Gilbert is a Cornish name, whereas Jilbert is French.

2. Larry D. Lankton, "Paternalism and Social Control in the Lake Superior Copper Mines, 1845-1913", *Upper Midwest History*, 5, (1985), pp. 1-2.

3. For details of construction and storms, see W. B. Frue, "Brief Sketch of Silver Islet", supplement to Silver Mining Company of Silver Islet, *Annual Report*, (New York, 1874), pp. 16-18. Financial and inventory data come from *Annual Report*, (1874), pp. 6-8, 10, and from McKellar, *Mining on the North Shore*, (1874), pp. 12-14.

Chapter 7
Earning Frue a Bonus (pages 41-43)

1. *Toronto Globe*, 21 August 1871.

2. Macfarlane, "Silver Islet" (1880). p. 248.

3. Frue Letterbook; Frue to Ed Trowbridge, 26 October 1871.

Chapter 8
Claimjumper! (pages 44-51)

1. *Ingall's Report* (1888), p. 4OH; for details of ore treatment see W. M. Courtis, "The Wyandotte Silver Smelting and Refining Works", *Transactions of the American Institute of Mining Engineers*, v. 2, (1873-4), pp. 89-101.

2. Janey C. Livingstone, *Historic Silver Islet: The Story of a Drowned Mine*, (Fort William, c1919), p. 7.

3. *Blue's Report* (1897), p. 143.

4. Sibley's Report (1873), n.p.

5. McKellar, *Mining on the North Shore*, (1874), p. 12.

6. *Blue's Report* (1897), p. 145.

7. NAC, MG30, A113; Philpott Papers, loose itemized statement of Silver Islet Mining Co. to Trowbridge, Wilcox & Co., 20 July 1872, in the amount of $ 844.53 .

Chapter 9
Of Mines and Mining Men (pages 52-56)

1. "Shuniah Lodge, A.F. & A.M., No. 287, G.R.C., Thunder Bay, Ontario, 100th Anniversary, 1872-1972", p. 7. The ten early members who gave their address as Silver Islet are James Bailey, W. H. Barlow, Albert J. Bowden, Lorne C. Campbell, William Currie, J. G. Gillis, William Mapledoram, S. Ridout, Thomas Trethewey and James W. Williams.

2. McKellar, *Mining on the North Shore*, (1874), p. 21.

3. Frue Letterbook; Frue to John McIntyre, W. R. Scott, Adam Crooks, and F. W. Cumberland, all dated 4 April 1872.

4. *Ibid.*; Frue to A. H. Sibley, 7 March 1872.

5. Donald McKellar, "History of the Post Office and Early Mail Service", TBHS, *Papers of 1912-13*, pp. 33-34; see also Keith Denis, "The Winter Mail Trail to Pigeon River", TBHMS, *Papers & Records 1973*, pp. 13-17, and Frank W. Campbell, "Minnesota as a Mail Outlet", supplement to "Northern Ontario Post Offices to 1895", (n.d.), reprinted from *B.N.A. Topics*, January-February 1948.

6. Frue Letterbook; Frue to John W. Cousins, 1 March 1872, and to A. H. Sibley, 19 March 1872.

7. *Ibid.*; Frue to Post Office Inspector, 24 June 1872.

8. *Ibid.*; Frue to Hugh Wilson, 13 February 1872; to A. H. Sibley, 19 and 26 February 1872; to W. A. Northrup, 26 February 1872.

9. *Ibid.*; Frue to Patrick L. Phelan, 4 April 1872.

10. J. McAree, "McAree's Narrative", Ontario, Bureau of Mines, *Annual Report*, (1899), v. 8, pt. 2, p. 139n.

11. Peter McKellar, "The Otter Head Tin Swindle", TBHS, *Papers of 1912-13*, p. 11.

12. Frue Letterbook; Frue to Hugh Wilson, 10 June 1872; to A. J. Duffield, 2 November 1872.

13. Lady Milton's influence on Fanny McIntyre is related in E. Marion Henderson, "Trousseau Treasures of 1872" in TBHMS, *Papers & Records 1984*, pp. 38-42.

14. Archives of Ontario [*hereafter AO*]; St. John the Evangelist Parish Registers, Baptisms 1873-1887.

15. Hariot Georgina Hamilton-Temple-Blackwood, Marchioness of Dufferin and Ava, *My Canadian Journal 1872-8, Extracts From My Letters Home*, (London, 1891), p. 169.

Chapter 10
An Image of Permanence (pages 57-67)

1. Frue Letterbook; Frue to Duncan Laurie, 12 March 1872, and to Walter McDermott, 19 November 1873.

2. Ruth Karen, *The Seven Worlds of Peru*, (New York: Funk & Wagnalls, 1969), p.67.

3. St. Andrew's Rectory; Official Register, volume 1B.

4. "St. Andrew's Catholic Church Centennial 1875-1975, Thunder Bay, Ontario", p. 14; see also *Dictionary of Canadian Biography*, v. 13, pp. 44-45.

5. Silver Islet Company, *Annual Report*, (1874), p. 11.

6. George McKanday, "A Short Life, A Long Memory", *Globe & Mail*, 4 January 1963.

7. Gertrude (Woodside) Dyke, *Historic Silver Islet*, (Thunder Bay, Drake Graphics, 1979), p. 5.

8. For construction details, see Frue Letterbook; Frue to Sibley, 4 April and 16 May 1872.

9. George Grant, *Ocean to Ocean: Sandford Fleming's Expedition Through Canada in 1872*, (Toronto, 1873, reprinted 1970), p. 26.

10. Ontario, *Statutes*, 1873, 36 Vict., c. 50, "An Act to organize the Municipality of Shuniah, and to amend the Acts for establishing Municipal Institutions in unorganized districts."

Chapter 11
Under Management's Thumb (pages 68-70)

1. Ontario, *Statutes*, 1872, 35 Vict., c. 37, "An Act to establish Municipal Institutions in the Districts of Parry Sound, Muskoka, Nipissing and Thunder Bay."

2. AO, Attorney-General Records, RG4-26, v. 4, p. 75; J. G. Scott to D. D. Van Norman, 5 August 1873.

3. *Duluth Herald*, 19 June 1875.

4. Belle Dobie, "Extracts from Rev. D. W. McKeracher's [sic] Diary of 1873", TBHS, *Papers of 1920*, p. 14.

5. *Op. cit.*

6. *Blue's Report* (1897), p. 150n.

Chapter 12
The Sinking of the Shaft (pages 71-78)

1. Silver Islet Company, *Annual Report*, (1874), p. 13.

2. Frue Letterbook; Frue to Ed Trowbridge, 19 February 1872.

3. Rowe, *The Hard Rock Men*, p. 167.

4. Silver Islet Company, *Annual Report*, (1874), p. 11.

5. Frue Letterbook; Frue to A. H. Sibley, 15 November 1872.

6. *Ibid.*, Frue to E. A. Trowbridge, 30 July 1873.

7. *Ibid.*, Frue to William Savard, 30 July 1873.

8. *Ibid.*; Frue to E. A. Trowbridge, 30 July 1872.

9. Macfarlane, "Silver Islet" (1880), p. 249.

Chapter 13
Industry in Transition (pages 79-85)

1. Dianne Newell, *Technology on the Frontier: Mining in Old Ontario*, (Vancouver: University of British Columbia Press, 1986), p. 21.

2. Frue, "Brief Sketch of Silver Islet", p. 21.

3. For his own description of developing the vanner, see Frue Letterbook; Frue to Walter McDermott, 19 November 1873; for an overview see *Blue's Report* (1897), p. 151.

4. For the local impact of the Frue Vanner, see Dianne Newell, "Silver Mining in the Thunder Bay District, 1865-1885", TBHMS, *Papers & Records 1985*, p. 40; for world impact, see Newell, *Technology on the Frontier*, p. 81.

5. *Ingall's Report* (1888), pp. 38H-39H; *Duluth Herald*, 10 June 1875; *Thunder Bay Sentinel*, 28 October 1875.

6. Macfarlane, "Silver Islet", (1880), p. 251; *Blue's Report* (1897), p. 152. The total milling cost of $5.50 a ton in *Ingall's Report* (1888), p. 38H, includes milling at $2.00 as well as mining, sorting and transportation to the mill.

7. Newell, "Silver Mining", p. 40.

8. *Ingall's Report* (1888), p. 36H.

Chapter 14
The End of an Era (pages 86-87)

1. Canada, *Sessional Papers*, (1876), "Number and Tonnage of Canadian and U. S. Vessels Entered Inward and Outward", p. 687.

2. "Press Excursion" in *Canadian Champion and County of Halton Intelligencer* (Milton, Ontario), 23 July 1868.

3. Jim Sigurdson, "Lighthouse of Doom", TBHS, *Papers of 1967*, pp. 9-11.

4. For particulars see Peter McKellar, "How Nepigon Bay Lost the C.P.R. Shipping Port on the Great Lakes", TBHS, *Papers of 1911-12*, pp. 25-7. The petition is titled "The Question of the Terminus of the Branch of Pacific Railway North Shore of Lake Superior", (Ottawa., 1874).

Part IV
A Quarter of a Mile Underground

Chapter 15
A Search for New Directions (pages 93-96)

1. Newell, "Silver Mining", pp. 40-1.

2. TBHMS; Diamond Drill Record.

3. *Blue's Report* (1897), pp. 152-4; *Thunder Bay Sentinel*, 23 November 1876; Livingstone, *Historic Silver Islet*, p. 22.

4. *Blue's Report* (1897), p. 153.

5. *Ibid*.

6. Silver Islet Consolidated Mining and Lands Company, *Annual Report*, (New York, 1879), pp. 1-5.

7. *Ibid*., p. 9.

8. *Ibid*., pp. 5-6.

Chapter 16
Bonanza at Last (pages 97-100)

1. *Ingall's Report* (1888), pp. 33H-34H.

2. *Ibid*., p. 27H.

3. Macfarlane, "Silver Islet", p. 236.

4. *Ingall's Report* (1888), p. 27H.

5. T. L. Tanton, *Fort William and Port Arthur, and Thunder Cape Map-Areas, Thunder Bay District, Ontario*, Memoir 167, (Canada, Geological Survey, 1931), p. 101.

6. *Thunder Bay Sentinel*, 28 October 1875.

7. Macfarlane, "Silver Islet", (1880), pp. 241-2, quoting a letter from W. B. Frue dated 28 January 1876.

8. *Ingall's Report* (1888), p. 28H.

Chapter 17
Life and Death Matters (pages 101-106)

1. J. C. Hamilton, *The Prairie Provinces, Sketches of Travel From Lake Ontario to Lake Winnipeg...*, (Toronto, 1876), as reprinted in Elizabeth Arthur, *Thunder Bay District 1821-1892: A Collection of Documents*, (Toronto, Champlain Society, 1973), p. 232.

2. Livingstone, *Historic Silver Islet*, p. 7.

3. AO, Colonization Roads Papers; C. F. Aylsworth to R. W. Scott, 25 October 1873.

4. Keith Denis, "The Winter Mail Trail to Pigeon River", TBHMS, *Papers & Records 1973*, p. 15.

5. Both TBHMS and Lakehead University Library Archives hold original copies of "Constitution and By-Laws of the Silver Islet Employees Benefit Society Established Sept. 1st, 1880", (Stratford, Ontario, 1880).

6. *Thunder Bay Sentinel*, 5 November 1880.

Chapter 18
Countdown Time (pages 107-111)

1. Woodstock Letters, v. 5, p. 60; extract from a letter signed by the Jesuit "E. R.", dated 24 October 1875.

2. Marquess of Lorne, *Canadian Pictures Drawn With Pen and Pencil*, (London, 1885), p. 134.

3. *Thunder Bay Sentinel*, 29 July 1881.

4. AO, Colonization Roads Papers (1882); #103, "Plan of the Village of Silver Islet and Silver Islet Mine, Silver Islet Consolidated Mining and Lands Company [1881]".

5. Tanton, Memoir 167, (1931), p. 93.

6. *Blue's Report* (1897), pp. 155-6 outlines the details of the mine's winddown.

7. Silver Islet Consolidated Company, *Annual Report*, (1884), p. 5.

8. *Blue's Report* (1897), p. 157.

9. Silver Islet Consolidated Company, *Annual Report*, (1884), p. 1.

Part V
Epilogue

Chapter 19
Aftermath (pages 114-120)

1. Elinor Barr, "The Port Arthur, Duluth & Western Railway 1883-1902: A Key Factor in the Development of the City of Thunder Bay", unpublished manuscript, pp. 6-20.

2. *Ingall's Report* (1888), p. 37H.

3. TBHMS; Diamond Drill Record.

4. Tanton, Memoir 167, (1931), pp. 95-6.

5. *Ibid.*, p. 104.

6. Information about the ownership and fate of the *Silver Spray* comes from John Mills of Toronto. In 1979 the Steamboat Historical Society of America published his extensive research under the title *Canadian Coastal and Inland Steam Vessels*.

7. N. L. Bowen, "Silver in Thunder Bay District", Ontario, Department of Mines, *Annual Report*, (1911), v. 20, pt. 1, p. 132.

8. *Engineering and Mining Journal*, 8 September 1888, p. 202; 22 September 1888, p. 246.

9. *Ibid.*, 12 July 1890, p. 57.

10. *Thunder Bay Sentinel*, 24 October 1891.

11. Ontario, Bureau of Mines, *Annual Report*, (1894), v. 3, pp. 72-4.

12. Ontario, Department of Mines, *Annual Report*, (1921), v. 30, pt. 1, p. 80.

13. *Port Arthur News Chronicle*, 23 January 1967.

14. Ontario, Department of Mines, *Annual Report*, (1934), v. 43, pt. 1, "Table X-Silver Shipments by Camps, 1904-1932", p. 17.

15. Tanton, Memoir 167, (1931), pp. 93-5.

16. Philip Smith, *Harvest From the Rock: A History of Mining in Ontario*, (Toronto: Macmillan, 1986), p. 55n.

Chapter 20
Nostalgia That Lingers (pages 121-129)

1. Christina Maude Livingstone, "Silver Islet: The Romance of a Lost Mine", *Fort William Daily Times Journal*, 17 April 1908.

2. Lakehead University Library Archives; Ross Matthews, "Oft in the Stilly Night", (n.d.), pp. 22-4.

3. *Fort William Daily Times Journal*, 15 August 1908.

4. NAC, MG30, A113; Philpott Papers.

5. "John McPherson Lifts Curtain on Early Days Here", *Fort William Daily Times Journal*, 14 April 1934.

6. *Ibid.*, 21 May 1910.

7. The story of this Danish settlement is told in *50 Years With Pass Lake Homesteaders 1924-1974*, 22 pages.

8. *Sibley Provincial Park, Master Plan*, (Ontario, Ministry of Natural Resources, 1980), p. 3.

9. Elliott Burden, *The Silver Islet Cemetery: A Survey and Description*, (Ontario, Ministry of Natural Resources, 1973) offers a study of the site.

10. NAC, MG30, A113; Philpott Papers.

RECOMMENDED READING

For further reading about Silver Islet, we recommend the following books:

CONFESSIONS OF A CORNISH MINER: SILVER ISLET 1870-1884
by James Strathbogey
Porphry Press
Thunder Bay, 195 pp

GEOLOGY AND SCENERY: NORTH SHORE OF LAKE SUPERIOR
by E. G. Pye, 1969
Ontario Department of Mines
Toronto, 144 pp

GHOST TOWNS OF ONTARIO: VOLUME 2
by Ron Brown, 1983
Cannonbooks
Toronto, 174 pp

HARVEST FROM THE ROCK: A HISTORY OF MINING IN ONTARIO
by Philip Smith, 1986
Macmillan
Toronto, 346 pp

HIGHWAY OF DESTINY: AN EPIC STORY OF CANADIAN DEVELOPMENT
by Joseph Placide Bertrand, 1959
Vantage
New York, 301 pp

HISTORIC SILVER ISLET
by Gertrude (Woodside) Dyke, 1979
Drake Graphics
Thunder Bay, 16 pp

A HISTORY OF THUNDER BAY: THE GOLDEN GATEWAY OF THE GREAT NORTHWEST
by Joseph M. Mauro, 1981
The City of Thunder Bay
Thunder Bay, 400 pp

THE McKELLAR STORY: McKELLAR PIONEERS IN LAKE SUPERIOR'S MINERAL COUNTRY, 1839-1929
by E. Marion Henderson, 1981
McKellar General Hospital Auxiliary
Thunder Bay, 161 pp

MADELEINE
a play by Laurent Goulet, 1982
Playwrights Canada
Toronto, 96 pp

NANNA BIJOU
by Jocelyne Villeneuve, 1981
Penumbra Press
Moonbeam, Ontario, 46 pp

OFF WATCH: TODAY AND YESTERDAY ON THE GREAT LAKES
by Anna Young, 1957
Ryerson
Toronto, 166 pp

SARAH JANE OF SILVER ISLET
a children's novel by Elizabeth Kouhi, 1983
Queenston House
Winnipeg, 144 pp

SILVER UNDER THE SEA: THE STORY OF THE SILVER ISLET MINE
by Helen Moore Strickland, 1979
Highway Book Shop
Cobalt, 244 pp

SUPERIOR: THE HAUNTED SHORE
by Wayland Drew, 1975
Gage
Toronto, 176 pp

THE SUPERIOR WAY: A CRUISING GUIDE TO LAKE SUPERIOR
by Bonnie Dahl, 1981
Inland Sea Press
Ashland, Wisconsin, 244 pp

TALES OF NANABOZHO
by Dorothy M. Reid, 1963
Oxford Universiy Press
Toronto, 128 pp

CREDITS

Illustrations, Tables, Maps

Cover Islet-Man-1880, Photographed by J.A.S. Esson, Prescott, Ont. F1132 Cumberland Papers, Ontario Archives (ST. 1232), Ontario Archives: 80 (ST.1244), 81 (ST.1242), 83 (ST.1237); Canada, Geological Survey, *Report of Progress*, Coste (1887): 116; Canada, Geological Survey, *Report of Progress*, Ingall (1888): 28, 115-I; J.E. Coslett: 124, 129; Bob Faithfull: 45-3, 46, 76, 95, 97; Frue Letterbook: 78; Geological Survey of Canada: 20 (202253); Grant, *Ocean to Ocean* (1873, 1970): 18\19 & 32; Lakehead University Archives 104 (Archive 38d); 104 Livingstone, *Historic Silver Islet* (c1919): 8\9, 62-1, 62-2, 63, 64-1, 64-2, 82; Macfarlane, "Silver Islet" (1879-80): 31, 84; McKellar, *Mining on the North Shore* (1874): 49; Metropolitan Toronto Library Board: 17, 23; National Archives of Canada: 88\89 & 107 (PA51166), 119 (PA15956), front endpaper (NMC3072), back endpaper (NMC5183, PA15957); Ontario, Bureau of Mines, *Annual Report*, Blue (1897): 36, 72, 98, 105; Roland, *Algoma West* (1887): 11; St. Andrew's Roman Catholic Church: 60-1; Sandra Saxberg: 128; Silver Mining Company of Silver Islet, *Annual Report* (1874): 50-1, 50-2, 51, 65; *Souvenir of Silver Islet*, (1913): 125; Strickland, *Silver Under the Sea*: 60-2, 85; Tanton, *Transactions* (1920): 16; Thunder Bay Historical Museum Society: cover (972.2.453), 34\35 & 58 (988.59.29), 41 (972.2.454), 45-1 & 45-2 (B25\2\1-2), 47 (975.1.47D), 59 (973.27.33), 61 (B25\1\1), 66 (972.3.15), 74 (972.2.342), 81 (972.4.6), 90 (981.39.215), 94 (972.2.345), 103 (976.110.93), 104 (B25\7\10), 108 (984.33.1B), 112\113 & 127 (974.2.528), 122 (981.38.60), 126 (973.27.32); Wilson, "Silver Islet" (1986): 99, 115-2.

CHRONOLOGY

1845   copper mining begins on south shore of Lake Superior
Canadian mining regulations passed, 27 licences issued including
Woods Location

1846   William Logan, Geological Survey of Canada, scouts north shore
John MacNaughton , government surveyor, lays out locations.
Montreal Mining Company hires Forrest Shepherd to inspect its
    Lake Superior locations and A. Wilkinson to survey them

1847   Montreal Mining Company incorporated

1855   Sault Ste. Marie canal opens
mines on south shore ship 3,000 tons of copper ore

1856   Montreal Mining Company patents Woods Location

1865   McKellar brothers discover Enterprise Mine (lead)

1866   Peter McKellar discovers Thunder Bay Mine (silver)

1867   Confederation of Canada
St. Ignace lighthouse built, first on Lake Superior

1868   Montreal Mining Company hires Thomas Macfarlane to inspect its
    Lake Superior locations
10 July silver vein discovered on Silver Islet
regular steamship service begins from Collingwood

1869   Geological Survey of Canada explores northwest shore
shaft sunk and shafthouse built on Silver Islet

1870   14 tons of ore worth $28,000 extracted 1868-70
Wolseley Expedition passes through to Red River
1 September Montreal Mining Company sells Woods Location to
    William Frue and Major A.H. Sibley
31 August Frue and workers arrived at Silver Islet, begin to build
    breakwater
before freezeup wives and children arrive, also a Methodist minister
Major Sibley visits
78 tons of ore extracted from open pit before freezeup

1871   buildings constructed on mainland and on the Islet
first bonanza
July open pit closed and underground mining begins
1 July smelter opens at Wyandotte near Detroit, processes 486 tons
    of ore by year end
Frue invests in tin mine at Otter Head

	21 December Sibley discovers claimjump attempt
1872	underwater vein traced by deep sea diver
	Burleigh drill and air compressor brought in
	Ontario Mineral Lands Company formed, Toronto
	Silver Mining Company of Silver Islet formed, New York
	June, John Livingstone arrives as customs inspector
	Frue sends men to work Jack Fish Mine (gold)
	2 titled Britons visit with a view to investing
1873	Father Baxter builds St. Rose of Lima Roman Catholic Church
	Thomas Macfarlane hires miners from Norway
	Ontario legislation creates Municipality of Shuniah
	School section and Board of Health established
1874	Governor General Lord Dufferin visits Silver Islet
	Sibley township surveyed
	October 26 Frue patents Frue Vanner
1875	May, stamp mill on mainland begins operations
	August 1 Frue resigns, Richard Trethewey becomes superintendent
	mine grossed almost $2million in silver 1870-75
	Silver Islet accounts for 70% customs revenues, Prince Arthur's Landing 30%
	sod turned in Westfort for transcontinental railway
	29 November diamond drill brought to Silver Islet
1876	Carl Oscar Wederkinch inspects mine, recommends inclined winze
	Silver Islet ore displayed at Philadelphia Centennial
1877	Silver Islet Consolidated Mining & Lands Company formed
1878	second bonanza
	Silver Islet ore displayed at Paris Fair
	Major Sibley dies, new president Edward Learned
1879	Dr. Tomkins dies, replaced by Dr. Lorne Campbell
1880	Silver Islet Employees Benefit Society formed
1881	shaft house built over inclined shaft
	Governor General the Marquess of Lorne visits
	Canadian Pacific Railway incorporated
1882	third bonanza peters out
	stamp mill gets up steam for the last time
1883	enginehouse explosion
	non-essential items sold
	shaft extends 1,250 feet underground
	Canadian Pacific railway completed to Red River
1884	March, pump stops and mine floods from within
	mine produced more than $1 million in silver 1876-84 for a total production of $3,250,000
	rise of Rabbit Mountain and Silver Mountain Mines
1886	Port arthur incorporated as a town
1888	Silver Islet's assets sold by auction in New York

1891	Silver Islet's assets sold by auction in Port Arthur
	first families camp at Silver Islet
1892	Falling price of silver closes Rabbit Mountain and Silver Mountain Mines
1893	stock market crash on Wall Street
	Presbyterian & Methodist churches sponsor picnic to Silver Islet with 500 participants
1902	Silver mine opens at Cobalt, Ontario
1908	Maude Livingstone's memoir published in *Daily Times Journal*
1910	Lake Coast Trading Company subdivides Woods Location as a summer resort
c1919	Janey Livingstone publishes memoir as a 24-page pamphlet
1920	Islet Exploration Company of Duluth reopens Silver Islet Mine until 1922
1924	immigrants from Denmark begin to settle in Pass Lake
1931	construction of road to Silver Islet
1936	Sibley Provincial Park designated
1967	Park becomes a natural environment park
1975	Q.C. Explorations Limited carries out extensive explorations until 1984

LIST OF TABLES

INDEX

"*n*" = foot note

St. Rose of Lima (see Catholic Church)

San Francisco (California) 109

Sandler, Robert 129

sandstone (see geology)

Sandy Beach 57, *57n*, 58, 123

Sault Ste. Marie (community) 42, 62, 86

Sault Ste. Marie (canal) 15

Savanne (Ontario) 87

Savard, Elizabeth Tamery Cole 60

Savard, William 60, 77

sawmill 87

Sawyer's Bay 14

Saxberg, Lorne 121

scarlet fever 63, 103

schoolhouse 58, 102, 121

   :teacher 58

   :trustees 68

schooner (see *Jessie*, *Whitefish*)

Schuyler, Chris 38

Scott, W. R. 48

scows 41, 42, 82

Sea Lion 125

Secord, Mr. 16-7

Sellers Point (see Catholic Point) *58n*

Sentinel (see *Thunder Bay Sentinel*)

servants 65, 102

Severance & Holt Company 93

Seymour, Mr. 47, 53

shaft 28, 73

   :inclined 100, 108, 114

   :vertical 94-5, 108

shafthouse 28, 42, 108, 119

Shagoina Island 14, 27, 117

Shebandowan Lake 33, 53

Shepherd, Forrest 14, 15, 17

Sherman Silver Purchase Act 118

Ship Island 117

Shuniah (name) 22

Shuniah Lodge 52

Shuniah Mine 22, 33, 52, 72

Shuniah, Municipality of 67, 68, 87

Sibley, Alexander H. 32, 33, 44, 47-8. 53, 55, 56, 57, 64, 68, 98, 101, 118, 128

Sibley, Frederick T. 118

Sibley, Henry H. 47, 56

Sibley, Henry Saxton 64, 118, 124

Sibley, Maria Louise Miller 64

Sibley, Solomon 47

Sibley Creek *57n*, 58, 64, 81

Sibley Peninsula 10, 11, 14, 16, 126

Sibley Provincial Parkl 126-7

Sibley Township 68, 126-7

Sifton & Ward 87

silver arch 96, 97, 107

silver brick 117

"Silver Gateway" 109

Silver Harbour Mine (see Beck Mine)

Silver Islet

   :name 26, 125

   :harbour 33, 65, 86, 87

   :island 10, 24, 121

   :mainland 11, 24, 27, 58, 94, 117, 121, 125

   :mine (see blacksmith shop, boarding house/s, breakwater, coffer dam, company store, customs house, diamond drill, dock/facilities, enginehouse, hoist, machine shop, ore cars, pumps, rockhouse, shaft, shafthouse, silver ore, warehouses, winze, Woods, Location)

   :ore/vein 10, 24, 26, 27, 29, 31, 39, 98, 117, 118

   :specimens 23, 101, 108

   :stamp mill 69, 79-84, 94, 95, 97, 109, 119 125

   :whistle 84, *117n*

Silver Islet Consolidated Mining & Lands Company 95, 114, 117, 118

Silver Islet Employees Benefit Society 103-6

Silver Islet Mining Company (see Silver Mining Company of Silver Islet)

Silver Mining Company of Silver Islet 48, 95

Silver Mountain 114, 118

silver ore 12, 14, 15, 16, 22, 55

   :packing ore 10, 71, 79, *79n*, 82, 97

   :stamp rock 71, 79, *79n*, 82

Silver Spray 41, 104, 108, 110, 114, 117

Simpson, George (HBC Governor) 14

Simmons, James 60

Simmons, John 38, 64

Simmons, Kate 64

Simmons, Margaret 64

skating 102, 117

skip (see hoist)

Skull Rock 24

Sleeping Giant (see also Nanabijou) 11, 14, 127

smelter (see also Wyandotte, Balbach, Swansea, Crooke) 44, 71

Smith, Tim 38

smuggling (see theft)

snowshoes 102

Sorel (Quebec) 117

sou'easters (see weather)

spiritus fermenti 69

stamp mill (see also Silver Islet) 22, 25, 29, 117

stamp rock (see silver ore)

stealing (see theft)

steamship (see also *Algoma, Cambria, Chicora, City of Detroit, City of Fremont, Doric, Forest City, Frances Smith, H. B. Tuttle, Islet Prince, Keewatin, Manitoba, Silver Spray* 42

Steep Rock Lake 119

store (see company store)

Strachan, Helen G. (see Cross)

Strachan, John 63, 114

Strachan, Catherine Stubbs 63

Stratton, Thomas 56

Strickland, Helen Marie 128

strike (underground miners) 72, 77

Stuart Location 23

Stubbs, Catherine (see Strachan)

sturgeon 125

Sullivan, J. T. 38

Sullivan, Margaret (see La Salle)

Sullivan, Martin 104

Sullivan, Paul 38

superintendent (see also Frue, R. Trethewey) 56

Surprenant, Mr. 28

*Note: The three profiles have been
indexed only under Macfarlane, Frue, and
Trethewey.*

ACKNOWLEDGMENTS

Although only one name appears as author of this book, a large number of people have assisted in its preparation.

Brent Scollie provided valuable leads about primary sources and notes from various documents. Brenda Cross shared knowledge of Silver Islet and its residents, her microfilm of the Cross Family Papers and also toured the cemetery with me. Peter Elliott contributed the period photographs he collected during filming of the documentary, "Rise and Fall of Silver Islet". Iain Hastie of Lakehead University designed the endpapers.

John Mills supplied data about the *Silver Spray* and other company vessels. Ted Leahy sent information about the Montreal Mining Company and Bruce Mines, and Marjorie Elliott deciphered Logan's handwritten journal. Others who contributed are Father Ed Dowling, S.J., Bernard Baxter, William C. Frue, Ann Drynan, Mabel Crooks, Bob Faithfull and Art Walker.

Of those caretakers of public documents who were involved, I would like to single out for special mention, Tory Tronrud of Thunder Bay Historical Museum Society, Vivian Nyyssonen Sharp of Lakehead University Library Archives, Susan Koski of the Regional Geologist's Office, Ontario Ministry of Northern Development and Mines, and Bette I. Clark of the municipality of Shuniah. I would also like to stress the importance of interlibrary loan to researchers like me who reside far from major repositories.

I am grateful for the care and attention given to reading the manuscript and for comments and suggestions by Dr. Elizabeth Arthur, Professor of History (retired), by George Patterson, Regional Geologist, Thunder Bay, and by Brenda Cross, genealogist and summer resident of Silver Islet. Nevertheless, errors that may have crept into the text are solely my responsibility.

Ted Scollie, Eric Fredrickson and Bill McKirdy assisted nobly with final preparation of the manuscript. Last, but not least, my husband Peter Barr has been a constant source of support and encouragement.

To the above people and institutions, and to others who have helped in a myriad of ways, I extend my heartfelt thanks and appreciation, and the hope that this book about Silver Islet Mine proves both entertaining and enlightening.

Elinor Barr,
Thunder Bay.

Elinor Barr has probably been interested in the past since moments after open-ing her eyes. She began writing for publication soon after graduating in history from Lakehead University.

In her writing and in her life she has become a fierce advocate of the culture unique to Northwestern Ontario, including the ongoing effort to restore and preserve Jimmy McOuat's log castle on White Otter Lake. Her first book, *Ignace: A Saga of the Shield*, was co-authored by Betty Dyck of Winnipeg and published in 1979 as the centennial history of their home town.

Since then Elinor has conributed entries to *The Canadian Encyclopedia* and *Dictionary of Canadian Biography*, carried out research for the National Film Board and TV Ontario's *la chaîne française*, and worked as photo researcher for the elegant *A Vast and Magnificent Land: An Illustrated History of Northern Ontario*. She lives in Thunder Bay.

Elinor Barr atop the Sleeping Giant, Silver Islet just out of sight upper left, 1994
Photo: Helen Smith, Thunder Bay.